Cost Management and Control in Government

Cost Management and Control in Government

Fighting the Cost War Through Leadership Driven Management

Dale R. Geiger

CMA CGFM

Cost Management and Control in Government: Fighting the Cost War Through Leadership Driven Management

Copyright © Business Expert Press, LLC, 2010.

First published in 2011 by
Business Expert Press, LLC
222 East 46th Street, New York, NY 10017
www.businessexpertpress.com

ISBN-13: 978-1-60649-217-8 (paperback)

ISBN-13: 978-1-60649-218-5 (e-book)

DOI 10.4128/9781606492185

A publication in the Business Expert Press Managerial Accounting collection

Collection ISSN: 2152-7113 (print)
Collection ISSN: 2152-7121 (electronic)

Cover design by Jonathan Pennell
Interior design by Scribe Inc. (www.scribenet.com)

First edition: May 2011

10 9 8 7 6 5 4 3 2 1

Printed in the United States of America.

Abstract

Government organizations spend enormous amounts. They employ a large percentage of the workforce. They have an undeniably huge impact on the national economy and wealth. Yet they are, for the most part, unmanaged.

What passes for management is a combination of oversight and audit. Oversight is primarily reactive: offering negative feedback for failures and demanding additional rules and regulations to prevent reoccurrences. Audits look for "bright line" discrepancies and clear violations to those rules and regulations. Working in tandem, these processes provide indignant sound bites and the appearance of management that is really mindless compliance to rules.

Government operations are often criticized for "waste and mismanagement." Yet the current situation, unfortunately, can best be described as one of "unmanagement" rather than "mismanagement."

Government can run better. It can run much better. The purpose of this book is to look at how government can move from "rule driven" to "leadership driven" management. Specifically, it documents and discusses specific examples of successful cost informed decision making and cost management and control in government. It also delineates the requirements of such success and explores the special needs of transforming the management culture of government from its well embedded past practices to a new paradigm of leadership driven management.

Society should be interested in better management in government, a huge component of the gross domestic product. Lower costs of government services mean that more services can be provided. For example, lower costs of national security mean that more security can be provided for the same budget. Similarly, lower costs of social welfare programs mean that more social welfare can be provided for the same budget. In the long run, of course, more efficient operations can result in reduced government debt and/or taxation, improving international competitiveness.

Keywords

Cost management, cost control, government management, Anti-Deficiency Act, ACE (analytic cost expert), cost war, budget, budget deficit, deficit reduction, organization based control, role based control, output based control, cost benefit analysis, cost managed organizations, leadership driven management, managerial costing, cost accounting, Fort Huachuca, continuous improvement

Contents

Blending People, Process, and Tools to Win the Cost War

A Genuine Recipe for Success

Dr. Linda Morrison Combs

Dr. Dale Geiger, in this book, presents one of the most complete, compelling, and persuasive recipes for success in controlling costs in the Federal Government. He challenges leaders at every level to become engaged in the war on costs through proven processes and methodology cited throughout this thought-provoking book. Leaders in the Federal Government constantly spring up at all levels and, when given the opportunity and latitude, can often cut through budgets, cost information, and organizational bureaucracy to make sense of "where the money is going." These leaders want to do the right thing. Dr. Geiger's case studies and templates can turn their desires into reality.

This book, through the use of real case studies, is about a natural blend of leading people; instituting good processes, methodologies, and tools; and includes a heavy dose of "common sense." Dr. Geiger's templates are designed to include an often overlooked asset—employee and team intellect. This is a gourmet recipe for bringing forth insight from the current mumbo jumbo found in most line units as well as many financial offices. Most of all, it provides a pathway that would bring about a much-needed culture change in Federal Government Departments and Agencies.

I have had the good fortune of working in six different Federal Government Agencies and Departments over the years in my Federal career.

In each and every one of these positions, trimming the cost of operations was viewed as critical, and many of my direct reports wanted to see cost trimming of our operations as much as I did. But seldom did we have the people, processes, tools, or culture necessary to make even rudimentary cost measurement a reality.

Every day thousands of Federal Government employees go to work. These men and women are most frequently dedicated and devoted to their organizations. These dedicated men and women are in every Department and Agency and at every level of the organization. But they have seldom, if ever, been challenged to trim costs in their organizations. They are challenged instead, as Dr. Geiger points out, to spend the money given to them. These dedicated men and women, if given an appropriate "cost trimming" challenge, and the processes and tools to meet that challenge, could become leaders on the front line to winning the war against waste, fraud, abuse, and cost in the Federal Government. They deserve a chance to implement cost savings, and the American taxpayer needs to witness the results of their efforts.

In this book, Dr. Geiger describes how many of his tools, templates, and methodologies have been in use for more than 20 years in Federal organizations. So not only are they sustainable, but they have been improved on over the years due to lessons and expertise gained from each use.

The current and future use of cost management in the Federal Government is ripe for implementation and expansion. With the ever-expanding public awareness of the size and scope of the Federal Government—and the great need to curb costs in every possible way—Dr. Geiger's book is exceptionally timely. This book opens the door, paves the way, and offers an excellent recipe for success to every leader willing to move forward to improve—and, in many cases, INSTITUTE—cost management in the Federal Government, Department by Department.

Linda Morrison Combs (http://morrisoncombs.com) is the former Controller of the United States, Office of Management and Budget. She has held five Senate-confirmed positions, including Chief Financial Officer at the Department of Transportation, Department of the Treasury, and the Environmental Protection Agency. Dr. Combs has also held several positions in the private sector. She is currently a writer, a speaker, a certified executive leadership coach, and a corporate and nonprofit board director.

INTRODUCTION

Cost Management and Control in Government

This book looks at how government can manage costs better. Specifically, it will document and discuss specific examples of successful cost informed decision making and cost management and control in government. It will also delineate the requirements of such success and explore the special needs of transforming the management culture of government from its well-embedded past practices to a new paradigm of leadership driven management.

Society should be interested in better management in government, a huge component of the gross domestic product. Lower costs of government services mean that more services can be provided. For example, lower costs of national security mean that more security can be provided for the same budget. Similarly, lower costs of social welfare programs mean that more social welfare can be provided for the same budget. In the long run, of course, more efficient operations can result in reduced government debt, taxation, or both, improving international competitiveness.

Government workers generally share these goals. Most are dedicated to the missions of government. Hundreds of thousands risk their lives for those missions. Many could be earning higher salaries in nongovernmental organizations. Most would welcome the opportunity to increase their mission effectiveness, and few would not appreciate the opportunity to lower their personal taxes.

Cost effective government operation should be universally attractive while essentially apolitical. Who would not like the opportunity to improve the societal benefits of government or to reduce the burden of paying taxes?

Ben Franklin taught us that "a penny saved is a penny earned." This practical Yankee advice also highlights the fact that both saving and earning generate funds.

Earning is one way to generate cash inflow. Doing so occupies or employs most of us. Cash inflow for an operating government entity is generally a budget appropriation.[1]

Government organizations spend considerable effort and resources to get their appropriations. In many ways, this is like a marketing function. Significant time and attention is paid to crafting budget requests to convincingly demonstrate "needs" that "should" be funded. Considerable effort is also made to secure "OPM," other people's money. Existing budget levels are jealously guarded.

Government organizations typically devote little attention to Ben Franklin's advice concerning "the penny saved." Accounting and control systems focus on spending within the budget and on avoiding gross abuses of "waste, fraud, and mismanagement."

Leadership driven management offers a different approach to conducting government operations through better financial management and control that seeks to move the organization toward "working smarter." It can generate significant resources. It is self-actuated and does not require external approval. When institutionalized, leadership driven management continues to generate returns on investment indefinitely.

CHAPTER 1

Opportunities for Leadership Driven Management

Unknown to most people, strong financial control does exist in government. At the federal level,[1] Congressional Oversight Committees, Agency Auditors General, the Office of Management and Budget, and the Government Accountability Office all work hard in their role as watchdogs, protecting the public from acts of "waste, fraud, and abuse." The federal management control complex makes significant efforts and spends enormous funds to implement these controls.

Current controls are rule based, and the rules work like commandments of the "thou shall not" category, prescribing things that should not be done and listing penalties for violation. It is not the purpose here to critique the costs and benefits of these practices. We will assume that they are necessary and useful in preventing "sins of commission" and "mismanagement."

Unmanagement Offers Much Greater Opportunity Than Mismanagement

However, rule based federal management practice is mostly silent on what good management practice should do. The objective here is to explore cost management practices that *are not currently being extensively used* in government management. The potential savings and efficiency improvements from these largely unexploited management techniques may be significantly more important than currently used controls.

This is to say that "unmanagement" rather than "mismanagement" may be the greater problem and a tremendous opportunity. In a sense, then, we must also address "sins of omission" and consider what we should do proactively and aggressively to better manage government's fiscal resources and their role in accomplishing the work of government. This is not an accounting issue; instead, it requires strong leadership driven management.

The Current State of Rule Based Federal Financial Management

The generally accepted definition of good management in government is spending 99.9% of the budget appropriation. This is not necessarily bad as far as it goes. Prohibition ("thou shall not") of spending more than appropriated is a good thing. This strong prohibition against over-spending the budget provides the foundation for the effective existing budgetary control process.

The strong prohibition of overspending comes from the Anti-Deficiency Act. The Act makes it a criminal offense for federal agencies to spend more than appropriated. The Supreme Court has also made it clear that the Executive Branch cannot defy the will of Congress by spending less than budgeted.

Spending less than 99.9% of budget is diligently avoided at all levels of federal agencies. Significant effort is made to spend funds because

Spending-Performance Tradeoffs

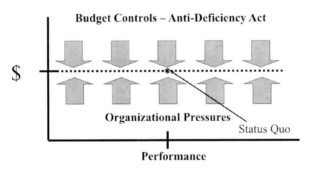

Figure 1.1. The twin pressures of organizational interest and the Anti-Deficiency Act mean that the budget gets spent regardless of performance.

unspent funds are "lost" to the budget holder, and reduced spending levels make it harder to justify desired budget increases in the future.

Figure 1.1 shows that the pressures to avoid overspending and underspending budget work to keep spending at budget levels. Budget controls and the powerful Anti-Deficiency Act mitigate against increased spending while organizational pressures strongly discourage underspending. These pressures are independent of performance. In other words, statutory spending requirements can be met and 99.9% of the budget can be spent at all levels of performance.

This current definition of good financial management is unsatisfactory, as it ignores how wisely the budget appropriation was spent. Good financial management should mean continuously improving the cost effectiveness of operations in ways that ultimately improve the overall effectiveness of government programs and missions. Figure 1.2 captures this management impact as an arrow driving increased performance within the spending constraint.

One very good Army garrison commander described the cost management and control process as being like sailing into the wind. Ships can sail into the wind only by adjusting the angle of the sails properly, steering at the correct angle into the wind, and tacking back and forth skillfully into the wind. However, he related that "as soon as you stop working the sails and let go of the rudder, the prevailing winds take over and you go in the opposite direction." (Colonel Mike Boardman, Garrison Commander, Fort Huachuca. See chapter 8, for more on the Fort Huachuca implementation of organization based control.)

Figure 1.2 labels this phenomenon as "drift": the natural tendency of people and organizations toward inefficiency and less challenging performance.

Conflicted Roles in Rule Based Management Practice

Rule based management processes do well in relatively simple matters but suffer when complex judgment is required. For example, traffic laws can prescribe the rules of the road. They can mandate speed limits, required stops, and even specified levels of equipment maintenance. Penalties exist for noncompliance (if caught violating) by traffic police (at a cost). The rules, however, cannot prevent lapses in judgment or ensure safe driving.

Spending-Performance Tradeoffs

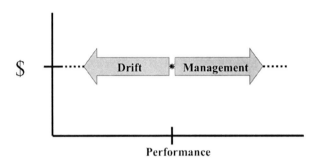

Figure 1.2. At any given spending level, there is a tension between the natural "drift" of organizations toward lower performance and the offsetting goal of management to increase it.

The nature of rule based processes creates a conflicting role for the rule making power in government. Consider the role of Congress in financial management and control. It holds the purse strings and it sets the rules.

The historical, constitutional role of a rule maker such as Congress is as a check and balance to the power of the Executive Branch. Congress uses its hearings, its budget and appropriation authority, and its Government Accountability Office and Congressional Budget Office to influence spending by Executive Branch agencies. Fulfilling this role generally results in an arm's length, sometimes adversarial, approach in which Congress exercises its oversight powers. Figure 1.3 shows Congress balancing the power of Executive Branch departments A, B, C, and D.

However, financial behavior of the Executive Branch is not independent of Congress. Congress is an integral and essential part of the financial management process in three ways.

First, Congress is solely responsible for appropriating the budget. The Executive Branch proposes and Congress disposes. Second, Congress has passed strict laws to ensure that the budget levels it appropriates are not overspent. Its Anti-Deficiency Act makes overspending the budget a criminal action punishable by fines and imprisonment. Third, it has been established that the Executive Branch is not permitted de facto budget setting power by neglecting to spend funds appropriated by Congress.

Congress as Check and Balance

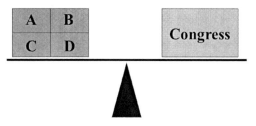

Figure 1.3. Congress (and often centralized agency headquarters) has a role to check and balance departments A, B, C, and D.

In this role, Congress assumes the top level of the financial management hierarchy. It is ultimately responsible for setting policies and funding outcomes. Hierarchies are common organizational structures, and the top of a hierarchy is usually recognized as the top management of that hierarchy.

Figure 1.4 depicts Congress at the top of the financial management hierarchy, providing all funding and direction to Executive Branch departments A, B, C, and D.

Congress as Top Management

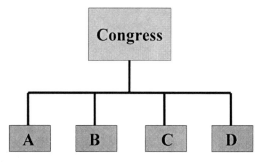

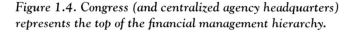

Figure 1.4. Congress (and centralized agency headquarters) represents the top of the financial management hierarchy.

These contrasting roles of checks and balances and financial executive are not unique to Congress. They are common to many government organizations. The Office of Management and Budget seeks both oversight and financial leadership over federal departments. Departments seek both oversight and financial leadership over their agencies, and so forth.

These contrasting, and somewhat schizophrenic, roles raise interesting questions of practical effectiveness. Yet Congress purports to be interested in resource consumption within the Federal Government. It seems to be the underlying theme indicated in the Chief Financial Officers Act and the Government Performance and Results Act.

Consider that the Chief Financial Officers Act states that "billions of dollars are lost each year through fraud, waste, abuse, and mismanagement among the hundreds of programs in the Federal Government. These losses could be significantly decreased by *improved* management." Similarly, a major objective of the Government Performance and Results Act is to "*improve* Federal program effectiveness and public accountability." Furthermore, the Federal Financial Management Improvement Act states that one of its goals is to "*improve performance, productivity and efficiency* of Federal Government financial management."[2]

These and other laws clearly indicate that Congress believes it has a role in improving the financial management of the Federal Government. Achieving this goal begs the question of whether the traditional checks-and-balances role is compatible with the leadership role.

Rule Driven Differences to Leadership Driven Management

Rule based management centers on laws, regulations, restrictions, and compliance audits. It appears similar to that of the legal process in which attorneys work in a rule driven, but adversarial, manner. The oversight process exhibits the dynamics of a legalistic approach. Evidence is sought and the jury of legislators, top managers, or the public is influenced. The goal of the process is to expose wrongdoing, and the process becomes inherently adversarial. Wrongdoing is most easily proved when actions are shown to violate established laws, rules, or principles: The success of this process requires rules and tests for compliance to the rules. These behaviors are common to the role of checks and balances.

On the other hand, effective management from the apex of the financial management chain of command would seem to require a more leadership driven approach. The leader, whether coach or captain, is part of the team. The leader, of course, must comply with the rules of the game. However, his role is much broader. Simply playing by the rules does not win the game. The leader must grow people, design processes, and deploy strategies to develop a winning team. There is not one way to do this. While every team plays by the same set of rules in any sport, there are many ways to play the game. The leader seeks to find the best combination of capabilities and opportunities to improve team performance.

Whereas the rule maker makes a rule, the leader makes a plan. The rule maker publishes the rule, while the leader trains personnel and teaches the plan. The rule maker seeks to prove or disprove compliance through an audit, and the leader tests the plan through interaction and review. The rule maker exposes wrongdoing in order to punish. The leader seeks to understand mistakes in order to learn from them. The rule maker penalizes wrongdoing, whereas the leader corrects mistakes and builds from what's right. The rule maker follows up by closing loopholes in the rules, whereas the leader evolves to a new and better plan.

Contrasting Managerial Dimensions

	Rule Driven	Leadership Driven
Goals	Follow the Rules Obey the Law	Increase Mission Effectiveness Though Increased Efficiency
Financial Accountability	Don't Overspend the Budget	Achieve Challenging, but Flexible Plans
Motivation	Negative – Avoid Punishment	Positive – Achieve Recognition
Information Systems	Comply to Reporting Requirements	Inform Management – Internal Reporting

Figure 1.5. The differing roles in rule driven and leadership driven management.

Consider four crucial dimensions of management: (a) goal setting, (b) accountability, (c) motivating, and (d) information systems (Figure 1.5).

The goal of an oversight process is to write comprehensive rules that, when obeyed, provide the desired outcome. Continuous process improvement, however, requires billions of efforts by millions of people because achievable improvements are embedded throughout the organization. Success requires a culture in which the goal is to increase mission effectiveness by improving efficiency. Such a goal appeals to dedicated personnel who have committed their lives and careers to the missions they manage.

Financial accountability is currently based on not overspending the budget. The current definition of good financial management in the Federal Government is to spend 99.9% of the budget. It does not matter how wisely it is spent, as long as spending does not exceed 100%.

Consider the budget mechanism as it relates to cost management. First, the budget cycle is relatively long. Management at the operating levels of federal organizations probably sees an 18-month period elapse from the time the budget is submitted until the budget year is over and the accounting process completed. Furthermore, no useful learning is possible because no variances exist. Everyone has worked diligently to spend 99.9% of the budget.

Worse, the budget process motivates spending in the fourth quarter to avoid underspending the budget. This motivation occurs at all levels of the organization. The Department level, of course, responds to the wishes of Congress to spend money appropriated as Congress has directed. Lower levels in the organization, however, seek to protect their budget levels by avoiding the suggestion that they could do with less.

No one wants to admit the budget is too high. Even if it is too high, who knows, maybe someone in the future will really need that budget, which brings us to the concept of *need*. Defining "needs" drives federal organizations. Many times managers have expressed interest in cost measurement, not to manage better but to express their needs better. We have created a culture that spends an enormous amount of time defining, defending, and, ultimately, denying needs when we would be better off spending some of that time continuously reducing needs.

The enormous effort federal organizations spend in defining their needs is particularly ironic, considering the underlying economic philosophy of the former Soviet Union: "From each according to ability: to each according to needs" resulted in similar overemphasis on needs and an underemphasis on developing abilities.

Financial management leadership requires a process of creating challenging but flexible plans throughout all levels of the organization. No learning occurs if plans are so conservative that they are always achieved; therefore, plans need to be somewhat challenging. This implies that missing a plan is not a crime. Accountability needs to be tempered with judgment.

Motivation of the federal agency in a legalistic oversight process is to avoid punishment. One unintended consequence of this type of motivation is that enormous efforts, and costs, are spent to avoid the negative. While leaders must sometimes use negative motivation, it seems clear that positive motivation has a very important role.

Adversarial processes are useful in the legal system in which plaintiff and defendant argue their cases and the judge or jury decides. It is harder to see the benefit of this style between a first-line supervisor and her workers or between a first lieutenant and his platoon. Although rank and hierarchy must be respected, cooperation may provide better results. The oversight process seeks to improve by exposing what is wrong. The leadership process seeks to improve by building on what is right while recognizing that perfect is the enemy of good.

Both styles create employee and organizational motivations. The oversight process motivates compliance. The leadership process should motivate creativity.

Information systems in the oversight process are directed at providing auditable information to the overseer. This external reporting process often requires considerable energy and expense. Highly defined and relatively rigid measurement processes ensure that consistency and auditability characterize external reporting systems.[3]

Continuous process improvement requires information that is relevant and useful to operating managers at all levels within the organization. This is an internal reporting process. Measurement processes for internal reporting systems emphasize fit and functionality and usually require significant customization to provide the needed functionality and credibility at reasonable cost.

Good financial management depends on sound general ledger accounting systems. Progress has been made since the Chief Financial Officers Act in establishing this foundation. However, it should be recognized that the job of these systems is to produce an aggregated external report once per year. Management information requirements for continuous improvement may be several orders of magnitude more detailed and more frequent. Furthermore, the existence of an auditable external report does not guarantee sound internal management. Most companies that file for bankruptcy have clean financial opinions.

Example of Dysfunctional Rule Driven Motivation: Budgetary Slack

To illustrate the motivational differences between legalistic and leadership modes, look at the common budgetary practice of building "padding" or "slack" into budgets. Slack is defined as the difference between spending plan and budget received. The criminal penalties of the Anti-Deficiency Act motivate significant slack.

Consider the position of a manager who faces criminal penalties for overspending the budget. Building in a safety margin of 10% or so would be very prudent. Problems may occur during the year that require funding. These can be funded from the budget slack, if available.

Significantly more difficult problems ensue if slack was not planned. Perhaps the organization could get additional budget by submitting a supplemental budget request. This may be politically difficult, if not impossible. If additional budget infusion is not possible, drastic spending cuts may be required. Contracts and staffs might have to be slashed quickly to cut funds outflow. These cuts might have to be made where possible rather than where best.

Consider, however, the impact in a five level organization if each level reacts to the legal threat by keeping 10% of its budget in reserve as slack. The top level keeps 10% and passes 90% down to its subordinate organizations. The subordinate organizations keep 9% (10% of its 90%) and pass down 81% (90% of its 90%) to their subordinates. Several similar cascades show the fifth level of the organization only spends 59% of the original budget (90% of 90% of 90% of 90% of 90%).

Hierarchical Slack

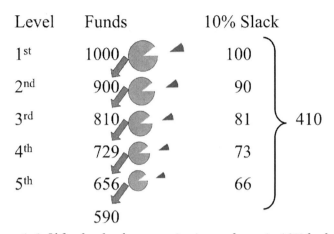

Level	Funds	10% Slack	
1st	1000	100	
2nd	900	90	
3rd	810	81	410
4th	729	73	
5th	656	66	
	590		

Figure 1.6. If five levels of an organization each retain 10% budget for contingencies, only 59% reaches the working sixth level.

Five levels that each build in a 10% safety margin create an organization-wide safety margin of 41%! (See Figure 1.6.) It should not be a surprise to learn that a lot of government spending occurs in the last quarter of the fiscal year as agencies scramble to spend all the left-over slack!

Imagine an alternative management philosophy based on the leadership model. Such a model might "capture" the huge slack currently used to defend against antideficiency violations. Once captured, that slack could be better planned to finance unfunded requirements and other programs designed to enhance the mission effectiveness of the organization.

Leadership Driven Management Opportunities

Government organizations can run better. They can run much better. The goals of this book are (a) to document practical solutions that have already been proven effective in government organizations and (b) to provide a framework for understanding the critical requirements for success in a simple theoretical framework in a manner that will help other organizations duplicate the successes.

Part I of this book will begin with *cost informed decision making*, undoubtedly the least complex and most obvious opportunity. Decisions, such as acquisition or policy making, usually involve a host of criteria. Cost is usually not the only concern, but any decision made in the absence of cost information will undoubtedly overvalue some other criterion.

- Chapter 2 will discuss the first and more important requirement for success: *aggressive, knowledgeable leadership*.
- Chapter 3 will cover the second critical requirement: *smart staff support*, costers, and cost analysts.
- Chapter 4 will show recent case examples of cost informed decision making from the United States Army Central Command headquartered at Camp Arifjan, Kuwait.

Part II will expand the complexity and persistence of cost usage that can be found in *cost managed organizations*. These organizations manage costs in a variety of ways that undoubtedly include multitudes of cost informed decisions made at many points within the organization. This is a very different management paradigm than that found in the budgetary control process. Experience has shown that several types of leadership driven management control processes are likely to be highly effective in improving the efficiency of government operations.

- Chapter 5 will outline the first additional requirement needed to move from cost informed decision making to a cost managed organization: an *interactive, learning oriented cost management process*.
- Chapter 6 will cover the second additional requirement needed to build a cost managed organization: *good cost measurement*.
- Chapter 7 will describe *organization based control processes* that drive cost management by relying on accountability relationships found in the organizational chart.
- Chapter 8 will present the 10-year-long case study of implementing an organization based control process at the Fort Huachuca Garrison.[4]
- Chapter 9 will describe *role based control processes* that seek to improve the efficiency and effectiveness of organizations linked

by their roles in a common purpose but not via an organization chart.

- Chapter 10 will present an application of this technique used to manage the roles and responsibilities of support functions for more than 15 years at the Navy's SPAWAR Systems Center Pacific research facility.
- Chapter 11 will describe *output based control processes* that use views of full or controllable costs to focus understanding and improvement on an organization's product or service.
- Chapter 12 will show the highly effective processes developed at the Bureau of Engraving and Printing to manage the cost of currency production for over twenty years.

Part III, the final section, will take a more futuristic view where appropriate elements of all previous chapters are integrated across the organization to build a truly *cost managed enterprise*. I know of no significant-sized government operation at this level of cost management maturity.

- Chapter 13 will discuss implementation issues of organizations facing transformation to improved cost effectiveness.
- Chapter 14 will close with conclusions.

Leadership Driven Management Lessons Learned

The idea of better cost management in government is not new. There have been numerous legislative attempts, as noted. Senior leaders such as U.S. Army Secretary Luis Caldera have also tried. (See Figure 1.7.) Unfortunately, most people in the Army did not "get the memo."

The hard-learned lesson, however, is that it takes more than paper to change entrenched management practices. Good management cannot be directed by memo, no matter how well written.

Good management must be leadership driven.

Successful implementation of a leadership driven management process requires four elements. Obviously, leaders are the highest priority of a leadership driven paradigm. Efforts to establish leadership driven management teach us that very strong staff support to the leader is also a prerequisite to success. The need for a "government-applicable" process is also clear. Finally, it would be hard to imagine a cost management process that did not need cost measurement. The reader who wishes to focus on these requirements should visit the following chapters.

1. **Aggressive, knowledgeable leaders** will be addressed first. These managers must understand the costs of their decisions and aggressively drive improvement (chapter 2).

2. **ACEs (Analytic Cost Experts)** are covered next. This staff runs the process while becoming the trusted financial advisors to operating management. It is arguably the most challenging requirement (chapter 3).

3. The **interactive, learning oriented review process** will then be covered as we move from cost informed decision making to interactive cost management processes that work through behavioral change. The workable process must provide an organizationally compatible, institutionalized forum for discussion, improvement of idea conveyance, and decision making (chapter 5).

4. The last requirement for success is **cost measurement** capability. Historically, this is the area that has received the most attention. In reality, little actually happens without managers to execute, processes to institutionalize and facilitate, and staff to analyze and advise (chapter 6).

Conclusions

It seems that the typical mode of management in government could best be described as a rule driven management process typified by *oversight*. Government oversight tends to be a centralized, rule driven, and somewhat legalistic approach. Congress exercises oversight of the Executive Branch. The Office of Management and Budget exercises oversight of the Departments. The Departments exercise oversight of their agencies and so forth down the organization structure.

Rule driven management plays a valuable, although limited, role. However, one definition of "an oversight" as a noun is "something overlooked or missed." Government management through oversight unfortunately overlooks and misses the opportunities offered by other management techniques.

Both rule driven, legalistic oversight and leadership driven approaches have advantages and disadvantages. The rule driven approach seems to make the most sense in checking and balancing. However, the limits of lawmaking and policy making seem to be substantial. If Congress or Agency level policy makers could significantly affect financial management practice by decree or legislation, we would probably not be having this discussion. If changing human behavior and interaction were so simple, we should also be able to rid ourselves of crime, hate, laziness, greed, and jealousy.

Rule driven oversight can only go so far in promoting better management. It seems to best perform the function of establishing boundaries. Significant improvement in federal financial management will likely require increased emphasis on a leadership driven financial management approach.

This book will provide examples of effective, government implemented cost management and control practices. Most significant, these examples have stood the test of time in their organizations. The goal of this effort is to propose some theoretical structure to these accomplishments and to evaluate critically the needed ingredients for them.

It is likely that history will have much to say about how the government of the United States has spent (often borrowed) resources over the last few decades. It appears illogical to assume that such behavior can continue indefinitely. It seems more likely that government resources will be increasingly constrained. Government agencies at all levels are likely to be embroiled in a Cost War: the struggle to accomplish their missions in an environment of constrained resources.[5]

While traditional oversight will always have its purpose, it is time to consider, fund, and implement leadership driven management processes. It is hoped that *Cost Management and Control in Government* offers some beneficial aid for fighting the cost war that far exceeds the cost of its reading.

SECRETARY OF THE ARMY
WASHINGTON

10 November 1999

MEMORANDUM FOR PRINCIPAL OFFICIALS OF HEADQUARTERS,
DEPARTMENT OF THE ARMY
MACOM COMMANDERS

SUBJECT: Strategic Plan for Implementing Cost Management/Activity Based
Costing (ABC)

In response to the USD(A&T) Memorandum on Defense-Wide
Implementation of Activity Based Costing/Management (ABC/M) dated July 9,
1999, the Army has developed the enclosed Strategic Implementation Plan. We
fully endorse Cost Management, using ABC where appropriate, as a process of
continuous improvement. The Army will pursue ABC as a tool for the local
manager to better understand operational cost and performance. We have an
aggressive goal to complete implementation in 11 major business areas that
support mission readiness within three years.

To meet this challenging timeline, we will provide ABC software and
sustainment, establish a Cost Management/ABC course to rapidly train each
business area, conduct prototypes in business areas as needed, and provide Cost
Management/ABC training material. Each business area will prepare and submit
detailed implementation plans through the Army Managerial Costing Steering
Committee. The Army Cost and Economic Analysis Center will provide detailed
instructions to each functional proponent in preparation for the upcoming steering
committee meeting in December 1999, with information briefings available upon
request.

Cost Management is not a one-time event; it is a long-term, continuous
process solution to control cost and improve operations. This is an important
culture changing event within the Army and must have leadership commitment
from each business area. We expect the fullest participation throughout the Army
and will monitor progress through the Quarterly Army Performance Review.

Louis Caldera

Enclosure

Figure 1.7. Secretary of the Army memorandum.

PART I

Stage I Cost Use
Making Cost Informed Decisions

Introduction

Anybody who has written a check mistakenly thinks they understand cost. Perhaps this is a good example of the saying "a little knowledge is a dangerous thing," because cost measurement can be a rich and complex endeavor. Accounting systems are good at recording transactions, and compulsory financial statements usually represent a standardized aggregation. Cost analysis, however, must isolate the relevant cost elements appropriate to a defined point of view, scope, and frequency.[1] This is generally not a standardized process but one that must be done with skill, understanding, and sound judgment.

Cost benefit analysis is arguably the most simplistic value-adding product of managerial costing. It simply represents an inescapable "law" of life that there must be a beneficial return on expenditure of resources. Hunting acquires food, conducting business brings revenue, working provides a paycheck. Who would make the effort if the costs/efforts of hunting, conducting business, or working were not to return a benefit?

Cost Informed Decision Making Defined

Horngren et al.[2] devote only two paragraphs to this in their 870-page popular textbook on cost accounting. They characterize it as follows:

> Management accountants continually face resource-allocation decisions, such as whether to purchase a new software package or hire a new employee. The cost benefit approach should be used in making these decisions: Resources should be spent if the expected

Cost Benefit Analysis:
The 1st Stage Role of Cost Use

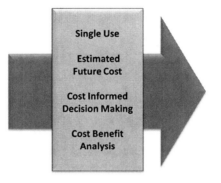

Single Use

**Estimated
Future Cost**

**Cost Informed
Decision Making**

**Cost Benefit
Analysis**

Figure 2.1. Cost information for cost benefit analysis is generally estimated and used by management for the sole purpose of making a one-time decision.

benefits to the company exceed the expected costs. The expected benefits and costs may not be easy to quantify. Nevertheless, the cost-benefit approach is useful for making resource-allocation decisions.

Consider the installation of a company's first budgeting system. Previously, the company used historical recordkeeping and little formal planning. A major benefit of installing a budgeting system is that it compels managers to plan ahead, compare actual to budgeted information, and take corrective action. These actions lead to different decisions that create more profits than the decisions that would have been made using the historical system. The expected benefits exceed the expected costs of the new budgeting system. These costs include investments in physical assets, in training managers and others, and in ongoing operations. (p. 12)

There are several distinguishing characteristics of this approach. First, we are generally looking into the future to tell whether anticipated benefits and costs balance. The future is not certain, so we make estimates. Moreover, if future costs, benefits, or both occur long into the future, they must be discounted to a present value (See Figure 2.1).

A typical investment decision involves a cost today and some anticipated investment return or benefit in the future. Assumptions (another distinguishing feature of cost estimates) must be made about the appropriate rate by which to discount those future benefits.

Another common feature of cost benefit analysis is opportunity costs. Consider the cost benefit analysis of going to school full time for an advanced degree. The opportunity cost of forgone income while studying full time could well be the major cost of the degree. The benefits used to justify this decision would be discounted future earnings in excess of what you would have earned had you not gone to graduate school.

Uncertainty about future events also plays a role. The cost of an investment is certain, but some risk is involved in getting a return. Consider a simpler example: the lion's hunt. The lion implicitly estimates the costs of a hunt. Those costs are calories and time. It must weigh the expected value of the benefit against these costs. Lions do not hunt rabbits because running after rabbits consumes a lot of cost compared with the expected food value of a success. They don't hunt elephants either for the same reason. Even though no running is required, there is a low expected value of benefit in attacking an animal so large and dangerous.

Lions learn cost benefit analysis or they do not survive. There is no "free lunch."

Cost Benefit Analysis Characterization

Cost benefit analysis ideally requires some quantification of cost and benefit. "Ideally" because benefits and costs are often subjective or judgmental. Benefits are often particularly difficult to quantify as benefits are often not expressed in dollar terms. There is often no correct answer on the value of the benefits. As "beauty is in the eye of the beholder," it is possible for rationale decision makers to make different assumptions concerning benefit value.

Costs typically are more tractable, although economists would argue that considering all externalities is required, and externalities can clearly be difficult to quantify. In many, if not most practical cases, cost can be reasonably estimated. This is valuable to the decision maker because such a cost estimate places a lower bound on the value that benefits must return to justify a decision. The decision maker can reach a conclusion much easier if he or she knows that value must exceed a minimum, cost based threshold.

CHAPTER 2

Developing Aggressive, Knowledgeable Management

Introduction

It is a popular notion of senior executives and officers to blame budget woes on the "bean counters" who make all the poor decisions and short change the important programs of government. If it is true that bean counters make key decisions, managers should welcome the opportunity to regain their rightful decision making leadership role. If it is not true, leaders should stop blaming others for what is inherently their responsibility.

As obvious as the importance of better financial management seems, the importance of developing leaders who are strong in financial management is often overlooked. Given the fundamental requirement of significantly greater financial accountability, this chapter seeks to develop ideas about the attributes of a good financial manager and how to develop those attributes.

There has been a long-term desire for better financial management in government that has resulted in a number of changes over the years. Although few management innovations are pioneered in government, the state of the art in government management has evolved considerably. The natural extension of this trend is a government management practice capable of implementing leadership driven management and control techniques.

Historical Perspective

The Anti-Deficiency Act may represent the starting point of the current trends in government management at the federal level. This Act responded to perceptions of excessive waste, fraud, and abuse. It imposed very strong controls to ensure that federal agencies did not overspend their budgets. The Act criminalized and personalized budget overspending with fines and imprisonment. These very strong penalties have since drastically influenced all financial processes.

While successful in achieving the goal of preventing spending more than budgeted, the Anti-Deficiency Act does nothing to influence "how" resources are spent. Policy makers and legislators certainly have impact, but the Federal Government is so large, and the view from the top is limited to big dollar issues and politically important areas. The vast majority of spending is more mundane and receives little oversight attention as long as the prohibitions of the Anti-Deficiency Act are observed.

The next era in the progression toward better financial management led Congress to implement the Chief Financial Officers (CFO) Act (1990) and the Government Performance and Results Act (GPRA; 1993). (See Figure 2.2.) The CFO Act established the chief financial officer position and ignited the decades long drive for audited financial statements.

Audited financial statements added significant new accounting requirements to federal agencies. The budgetary controls stipulated in the Anti-Deficiency Act required only the most basic cash accounting. The need for audited financial statements required enormous systems efforts and a lot more accounting attention. However, while audited financial statements certainly are a step toward better financial management, they fail to address "how" resources are spent. Companies with clean audit statements go bankrupt every day.

Clearly, more than good accounting is needed to reach the goal of better financial management. Congress hoped that the GPRA would meet the need. This Act sought to improve performance by linking budget to performance and calling for strategic plans and performance reports from agencies. In most agencies, however, compliance with the letter of the law was observed with a minimum of real change in the management process. Agencies found that high level staff could file required reports and answer obligatory questions. Thus both the CFO Act and GPRA can be thought of as primarily affecting and improving external reporting quality but, again, failing to influence the "how" of government spending.

That significant change in major agencies takes years to occur and even longer to observe meant that few high level political appointees had

Management Transformation Trend

Figure 2.2. There has been a trend of increasing interest in federal financial management improvement.

any stake in investing in real performance management. The next era in government management required political commitment from the Executive Branch.

Presidents Clinton and Bush carried government management into the next stage with their Reinventing Government and Presidential Management Agenda initiatives. Reinventing Government seemed adept at motivating and publicizing anecdotes of performance improvement but failed to connect the islands of innovation that sprang up. The Presidential Management Agenda took a more centralized view of seriously reviewing department level performance metrics using a "scorecard" approach but appears to have failed in energizing and institutionalizing commitment to change down to the lower levels of agency hierarchies.

Political appointees leading federal agencies took these initiatives seriously because the President took them seriously. The focus, however, is upward: satisfying the requirement. Not surprisingly, few political appointees, the leaders of federal agencies, appear willing to invest time and energy in implementing time-consuming reformation efforts that may take 10 to 15 years to achieve.

The net result in most agencies seems to be greater reporting of performance metrics with little practical change in the management culture. Furthermore, as the demise of the Reinventing Government initiative suggests, any presidential attempt at management reform is unlikely to survive the next change of administration.

Some progress, however, has been made and a good foundation exists for the next stage of governmental management: leadership driven management. Budget controls exist. Accounting quality and credibility have greatly improved. Political leadership is undoubtedly supportive. The stage is set for real change.

The stimulus for change now is more pervasive and persistent. It is based in the current fiscal environment. Limited fiscal resources create an environment in which better financial management is increasingly critical to accomplishing government's missions. Financing those missions through increased national debt or increased taxation faces political and practical limits. Furthermore, all missions are competing against resource needs to fight the global war on terrorism and to bolster the security of the homeland.

Let's visualize the role of managers in a leadership driven management process and differentiate that role from past practice.

The Emerging Role of Managers in Leadership Driven Management

Senior executives and officers were largely exempted from the requirements of the first four eras of government management transformation. They will be the key to success in the final stage. Congress can make laws but cannot drive sound management practice down through the layers of large federal organizations. Elected officials and the political appointees they bring may not have sufficient expectations of longevity to begin to be interested in long-term programs. It is the career civil service manager that will emerge as the primary actor in leadership driven management with critical support and direction from Congress and the Chief Executive.

We currently expect and historically have expected too little of government managers. The current state of government management can be described as centralized administration. Policies, goals, and budgets are passed down from the top tier of the organization.

Focus on the Tier 2 manager's relationship with the Tier 3 manager in Figure 2.3. In a centralized administration model, relatively little

Centralized Administration

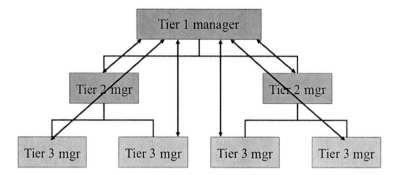

Figure 2.3. Once centralized management sets the budget, relatively little interaction occurs through the chain of command.

interaction occurs in the financial dimension between the two levels. Both comply with directives, rules, and restrictions from the centralized administration. These behavioral or action controls spell out "standards" for the entire organization and encourage little individualism in approach.

It is not surprising that "management" has a somewhat negative connotation, especially in military organizations. The Navy, for example, thought it necessary to rename *total quality management* to *total quality leadership* because many viewed management as a static, dull, mechanical, perfunctory process. This view of a weak role of management centered around compliance.

Leadership Driven Management

This management paradigm requires much more aggressive, accountable management skills.

Managers in a decentralized management control environment not only must meet or exceed the goals of their superiors but also must set goals for their subordinates and interact intensively with them. Contrast Figure 2.4 in terms of the interaction between Tier 2 and Tier 3 managers. This model uses the chain of command and places great importance on the Tier 2 manager to direct, motivate, and evaluate subordinates.

The key difference is that now the Tier 2 manager "answers" for all Tier 3 elements under his control. The accountability and responsibility of the Tier 2 manager is greatly increased. This relationship is extended throughout the lower levels of the organization. This change creates a much more accountable organization because managers at all levels are accountable to their immediate superior, who has frequent interaction, rather than to centralized authority.

Job Requirements

Success in improved operational control, indirect control, or output based control will not happen with the current expectations of managers. Success requires increased accountability and responsibility throughout the chain of command. Every manager *must* operate with the personal expectation of improved productivity, quality, customer service, and so forth, and expect subordinates to do the same.

Leadership driven management requires new and different skills. The basic issue is that leadership driven managers must spend considerably more energy leading their organizations' financial efforts. This also

Decentralized Management Control

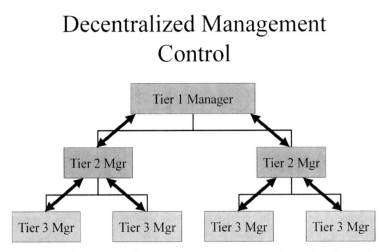

Figure 2.4. Leadership driven management strengthens the chain of command at all levels.

requires managers to develop their subordinates to lead financial efforts within the subordinate organizations.

Motivation Issues

One of a leader's most important responsibilities is motivation.

Budget controls, while effective in preventing overspending, have real problems motivating performance. In fact, they create problems. Consider an organization with two equal-sized branches where one improves performance and the other degrades performance. To bring the combined organization into compliance with the Anti-Deficiency Act, every effort will be made to take the efficient organization's savings and use them to fund the poor performance of the other organization.

Figure 2.5 highlights the problems in motivating performance in a budget-controlled organization.

What outcome is appropriate for an organization that improves performance? The alternative of rewarding that organization with more budget may not make sense if the organization has shown it can operate well with less budget. However, the alternative of shifting budget to

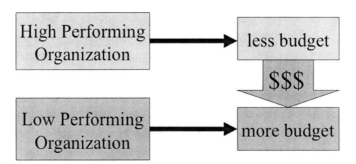

Figure 2.5. High-performing organizations are often perceived as not "needing" resources that are then shifted to low-performing organizations that "need" them. Consider the motivations of such a practice.

other more "needy" organizations clearly penalizes the high-performing organization.

The opposite conundrum also applies if an organization exhibits poor performance. That organization may actually be rewarded with budget resources proved by their "need." It is hard to imagine disciplining that organization with lower budgets.

This reward and motivation structure poses a great problem in motivating better performance. What can be done about it?

Clearly, budget outcomes must be disassociated from performance achievements. One way is to eliminate the budget control process so the expectations and entitlements of the budget process do not exist. This should reduce the importance of perceived "need" as the determinate of future budgets. Such an approach is too radical a change for entire agencies or departments but makes great sense at lower levels of the organization.

Most important, however, is a mechanism to separate outcomes that impact the organization from outcomes that impact the leader. Consider the poor-performing organization described earlier. Perhaps the best outcome would be providing more resources to the organization and firing the leader.

Meaningful Accountability Means Personal Implications Needed

It is interesting to note that the Anti-Deficiency Act made individuals personally accountable and subject to criminal penalties. It seems clear that poorly performing individuals must also have personal and significant negative outcomes for leadership driven management to succeed. Leadership driven financial management, however, can also offer positive motivations unavailable in the Anti-Deficiency Act. Leaders who consistently demonstrate their ability to improve financial performance can and should receive significant bonuses and see significant career enhancement.

For leadership driven management to succeed, managers must be accountable. At a minimum, this means that leader's performance measures must include a dimension of their organizations' financial performance. It will be taken seriously only when this is considered important enough to impact careers.

There is one other obvious way to improve effectiveness. Budget controls motivate the spending of resources in the specific areas where funds were budgeted. Cost effectiveness can be increased by simply allowing redirection or reprogramming of funds to where they would do the most good. On the other hand, organizations should never perceive a cause-and-effect relationship where improved performance leads to budget cuts. When budget cuts are made, they should be presented as independently driven by higher level issues so that they clearly are not perceived as happening as a result of good work.

Training Needs

Leadership driven managers must also assume full and unequivocal accountability for all dimensions of their financial results. This is a key point. Accounting staff may do the measurement, but ownership of the numbers is vested in the leadership.

Current government management training seems to ignore this point. Few master's degree programs in public administration or public policy offer even basic accounting electives. Fewer still have course requirements in managerial costing or financial control. Perhaps this should not be surprising, as political science departments run most programs of this nature.

Federal training for new senior executive service managers also seems to ignore the need for accounting understanding and results accountability. The curriculum for the Federal Executives Institute, for example, offers nothing on accounting or accountability.

Agencies seeking to develop leader's strengths in financial management and control might consider several mechanisms and techniques. Training can be thought of in two modes: (a) training for transformation and (b) training for sustainment.

Transformation requires the consensus of top leaders because they must lead the leadership driven management program. The busy chief operating officer and major organization operating officers probably can only learn the highlights of the leadership driven management paradigm through an off-site "retreat," for example. As a practical matter, they must rely on a strong staff to provide "on-the-job training." This will be covered in the next chapter.

Once top management has developed a consensus and understanding, the transformation program must be extended throughout the organization. One of the more effective training mechanisms is a hierarchical approach. The organization's operating manager briefs subordinates on key elements of the program and their responsibilities. Each subordinate uses the same briefing to train his or her own subordinates. The process continues throughout the organization until every manager, supervisor, and employee has heard the same thing. More important, they have heard it from their boss. It is also recommended that the boss attend the training sessions given by subordinates to ensure that the subordinate delivers the message properly. This is the first opportunity to evaluate that subordinate's willingness and ability to accept financial management responsibility.

This "chain briefing" approach can get the key ideas across while showing the organization that changes are expected. Additional skill development training should be available to enhance the ability of subordinates to execute the program. Numerous cost analysis techniques could be taught. Perhaps the curriculum of an MBA-level managerial accounting and control class would be appropriate. However, the time and cost of such a program probably make it prohibitive. Several important topics, however, should be taught.

Most important is the particular management control process that the organization has adopted. Managers should be familiar with the process and understand expectations from the roles of both supervisor and subordinate. Examples should be shown of managers' presentations. Mini case studies might be appropriate. Role playing would also be a useful training technique.

Some specific techniques may be taught based on the nature of the organization and its typical decisions. One that is universal and should be part of the core training process is cost benefit analysis. Managers should be sensitive to making tradeoffs between alternatives and between costs and benefits.

Another essential training requirement is the nature of continuous improvements. Anecdotes should be presented that demonstrate the creativity of employees and managers from similar organizations. Perhaps a mini case study could be used to stimulate a discussion about creative solutions.

Sustainment training programs will be similar to the transformational programs. However, their scope will be limited to employees new to the organization or promoted to positions of increased accountability. Transformation training is likely to be a relatively larger effort, with every manager in the organization participating in some way. Sustainment training will be supplemented by on-the-job training and is likely to be one-tenth as large. Mature organizations will have embedded cost control into all employee development programs in some way. For example, even employee orientation could be expected to include discussion of accountability and continuous improvement.

Training programs should be customized to the greatest extent possible. Revolving funded organizations, for example, might have entirely different emphases, including "profit" review. Project oriented organizations might include earned value approaches. Repair functions dealing with inventory and manufacturing organizations have another set of areas to cover. Customization also benefits learning by incorporating case studies relevant to the students that can also serve as examples of the possible and expected.

Succession Issues

The workforce often treats managerial change initiatives with skepticism. Senior leadership is sometimes labeled as "tourists" because their average tenure is often short. However, senior leaders often arrive with ambitious plans to distinguish themselves. Careerist agency personnel have learned that they need simply wait out the current leadership because the next leader will have new ideas. Far too often it also seems that new leadership throws out the previous administration's initiatives.

Leadership driven management control cannot survive without strong continuity. This has a number of implications. First, leaders must be briefed on their role in the management process before being offered the position. Their willingness, if not eagerness, to operate through a leadership driven management control process should be considered as part of the selection process.

Second, new leaders should receive sustainment training in leadership driven control techniques before assuming their responsibilities. Third, new leaders should also make it clear as one of their first actions that they value the leadership driven control process and seek new inputs to strengthen it and increase its contributions.

Succession issues are particularly critical during the 3-year start-up period of the process. Failure to sustain the momentum as management personnel change is perhaps the major threat to program success.

Conclusions

Use of cost information is a fundamental part of being a leader. Staff, consultants, and subordinates can make recommendations, but leaders cannot escape their inherent fiscal accountability because resources are inevitably tied to results. A corollary of this observation is that cost informed decision making, cost managed organizations, and cost managed enterprises cannot, and will not, occur without leadership driven management.

Better financial management requires better financial managers. The concept of being a good manager means different things to different people. A simple definition of a good manager (one often used in performance reviews) is "someone who meets or exceeds the organization's mission goals." A better definition might be one who meets or exceeds the continuous improvement goals of his superiors and sets challenging but achievable continuous improvement goals for his subordinates.

Some seem to think that good financial management is simply a matter of making good decisions. That model then attempts to provide data and decision support tools and formats to aid in the decision making process. Making good decisions is certainly better than making poor decisions. However, cost informed decision making should be thought of as a starting point in building cost managed organizations.

Cost managed organizations require an expanded role for leadership since subordinates' behavior is involved. Part II covers this expanded role in which the core requirement of good financial management is stimulating and leading change. Changing attitudes, behaviors, and processes is a much more complex and demanding process than cost based decision making.

The needed manager skills in the coming era of performance management are different from the traditional. Leaders must be able to drive the financial management and control processes of the organization. They must be able to understand and evaluate the achievements and, as importantly, the attitudes and accountabilities of subordinates in achieving improvement. They should be skilled in asking questions and bringing out the best in their employees. They should constantly signal the importance of improving operations.

Many of these skills will be underdeveloped in current leadership teams. Transformational training is needed to better equip leaders at all levels in their new, cost related roles. Cost savvy leaders are an absolute requirement of leadership driven management.

CHAPTER 3

ACEs

Building a Talented, Smart Support Staff of Analytic Cost Experts

Introduction

Even in the business world, few leaders started their careers with an exceptionally strong background in financial management and control. Most managers' careers started in functional areas, such as engineering, marketing, or manufacturing. As they advance from individual contributor to supervisory roles, they usually assume cost center management responsibilities.

Promotions from that point increasingly require cost management as well as functional expertise. By the time an individual reaches profit center or investment center responsibilities, he or she likely has decades of demonstrated cost management success. Corporate leaders are quite proficient in cost and profit management by the time they reach senior executive levels.

The financial upbringing of government executives is quite different. Currently, supervisors and managers have little, if any, need to get involved in cost details. As long as the budget staff reports sufficient unobligated balances, there is no reason to be concerned, except at year-end, when every effort is made to spend all outstanding balances. A good financial manager in government is simply someone who spends 99.9% of the budget.

This engrained situation makes it difficult to transform a government organization, particularly an appropriated one, into a well-controlled, continuously improving organization. Even senior managers are often "rookies" when it comes to the skill set required for success.

Corrective options would seem to be management recruiting, training, and development. These are certainly important and were discussed in the previous chapter. As a practical matter, however, while improving the skill set of management is desirable in the long run, transformation cannot wait for complete reeducation or repopulation of the management team. An exceptionally smart and talented support staff is needed to compensate for this deficiency. Furthermore, even the most cost and performance savvy managers would probably benefit from highly capable staff support.

Some organizations appear to "wish away" this problem. They seem to feel that management control is so easy that simply providing managers with cost data automatically leads to better cost management. The often painful lesson is that cost data do not guarantee success but merely enable it.

Cost data do not automatically become cost information. Too many try to produce good costing through expensive measurement procedures, such as activity based costing. What they often get can be thought of as "gee whiz" numbers because about all that happens is management says, "Gee whiz, it is interesting that it costs that much." Nothing else happens because there is no context for what the numbers mean, how they vary from expectations, and what implications they hold for action. Effort and skill are required to transform raw cost data into actionable management information.

Fortunately, these "intelligence" requirements can be provided to the management team by a competent analytic cost expert (ACE). Such staffers enable leadership driven management by distilling management-relevant information hidden in the mass of data. They must be able to convey the actionable intelligence contained in cost data to their supported leaders and help the leader develop appropriate decisions and actions that improve the organization's cost effectiveness.

Needed Skill Set

The ACE staff position requires many skills. Primary is strong analytic capability. The ACE must be able to delve into accounting data to distill management information. This is not as easy as it may seem, and, surprisingly, it is not traditional accounting.

Traditional accounting applies generally accepted principles and methods that provide a view of financial information consistent with similar views from other organizations. This can be thought of as external reporting, while the ACE seeks internally useful views.

Internally useful views of cost information need not be consistent with other organizations' views. It is possible that more than one useful view exists. Furthermore, managerially useful information often requires unique scope requirements and targeted techniques.

Consider, for example, opportunity cost. Opportunity cost is a very relevant information input to many management decisions, such as rent versus buy, infrastructure investment, or capital asset acquisition. External reporting principles are silent, however, on opportunity cost determination because it is not part of the generally accepted external reporting requirements. The ACE, therefore, must be able to take a broader view of cost accounting than is typically used by accountants trained for external reporting. We will label this broader view as managerial costing.

There is often a large degree of ambiguity in managerial costing that requires making assumptions about scope, fullness, and point of view. Making assumptions is simply an inescapable aspect of managerial costing. External reporting oriented accountants often prefer predetermined principles and are uncomfortable making assumptions.

The duties of the ACE include the following:

1. Understanding and explaining cost relationships
2. Analyzing and explaining cost tradeoffs
3. Planning and explaining future costs
4. Reconciling and explaining historical cost

General management education with strong math skills may turn out to be the best indicator of success as a managerial coster. General management background is useful because ACEs must be able to explain costs to operational management.

Understanding and Explaining Cost Relationships

Managerial costers must recognize the many managerially useful ways to measure cost. Cost accounting textbooks cover the following "flavors" of cost: direct, indirect, variable, fixed, sunk, period, inventoriable, reimburseable, capital, standard, conversion, prime, carrying, incremental, separable, joint, controllable, current, historical, discretionary, full, project, responsibility, imputed, normal, opportunity, mixed, out-of-pocket, relevant, target, absorption, average, quality, estimated, and unit.

ACEs must understand the variety of methods, select the appropriate one, and explain the selection and resulting cost information to management.

Understanding the algebraic relationship inherent in certain costs can be very helpful. For example, total cost can be expressed as the sum of fixed cost and variable cost. Variable cost can be evaluated as incremental unit cost multiplied by the number of units. Simple algebraic analysis and graphing show the following relationships of fixed cost, variable cost, fixed cost per unit, and variable cost per unit (Figure 3.1).

Analyzing and Explaining Cost Tradeoffs

Cost analysis is often useful in evaluating alternatives (Figure 3.2).

Consider a simple example in which two purchasing or perhaps processing alternatives exist. One has a fixed cost of $100 and a variable cost

Simple Cost Relationships

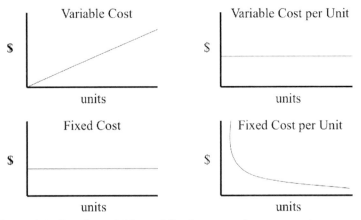

Figure 3.1. Simple variable and fixed costs and cost per unit relationships are basic to cost analysis.

of $2 per unit. The other has a fixed cost of $200 and a variable cost of $1 per unit.

It is relatively easy to determine the cost of alternatives at a planned loading of 50 units, for example. Alternative 1 costs $200 ($100 fixed plus $100 variable). Alternative 2 costs $250 ($200 fixed plus $50 variable). Alternative 1 is clearly preferable given the planned loading assumption.

Tradeoff analysis can also calculate the point of indifference. This can be done algebraically by solving for the number of units where the costs are equal.

$$\$100 + \$2 * units = \$200 + \$1 * units$$

$$\$2 * units - \$1 * units = \$200 - \$100$$

$$units = 100$$

Interpretation would show that Alternative 1 is a lower cost alternative for a planned loading level of less than 100, Alternative 2 is better for levels exceeding 100 units, and it does not make any difference when planned loading is 100 units.

Cost Tradeoffs

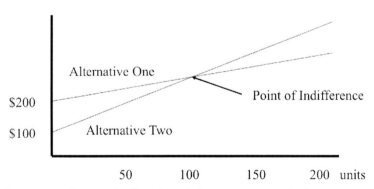

Figure 3.2. Cost tradeoff analysis helps managers make better decisions.

Planning and Explaining Future Costs

Projecting future cost is an important part of the control function, especially for cost informed decision making where cost and benefit tradeoffs are important. In cost managed organizations (Part II), projections are often the front end of the management accountability process because projections represent management commitment for future performance.

By their nature, projections also force leadership driven managers to think ahead. Thinking ahead is usually better than reacting. Thinking ahead enables aggressive, intelligent action to avoid pitfalls and to take advantage of opportunities.

The ACE staff should be able to help managers develop projections.

Reconciling and Explaining Differences From Projected Cost

Cost managed organizations (Part II) need staff who can help interpret differences between projected and actual costs. Perhaps the most important aspect of the management control process is the after action review. The accountability loop is closed in this meeting when managers explain actual performance in comparison to previous projections or historical cost.

The primary goal of the after action review is learning (as described in chapter 5). Managers need help with this process. While the managers are clearly the accountable parties, they need help in understanding their costs.

The ACE's role is to provide the technical expertise that researches actual results, describes those results in cost terms, and explains the situation to the accountable manager who then must present "his or her" performance to higher management.

Consider an example in which an organization spent $500 versus a spending plan of $400. The variance, or difference, to be explained is $100. More precisely, the variance is ($100), which should be read as "unfavorable $100." All variances are either favorable, implying good news, or unfavorable, implying bad news. Management's responsibility is to explain the variance, and the ACE support staff is generally required to help management determine that explanation.

The explanation will usually be a mix of favorable and unfavorable elements of importance and a lumping of "other" relatively unimportant impacts. A typical reconciliation might look like that in Table 3.1.

The goal of the reconciliation process is to tell the story about that period's performance. The story that emerges from the reconciliation example in Table 3.1 is that a major contract overrun occurred and management action to cut spending and delay hiring offset about half of the problem.

Structure

The organizational structure of the ACE managerial costing staff is extremely important. Having the staff organization parallel the management chain of command offers a number of advantages (Figure 3.3).

Table 3.1. A Reconciliation Example

Planned Spending	$400
Actual Spending	$500
Variance to be Explained	($100)
Reconciliation	
Contract Overrun	($200)
Delayed Hiring	$60
Spending Cuts Implemented	$45
All Other	($5)
Amount Explained	($100)

Cost Chain of Command

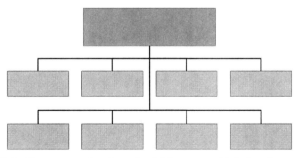

Figure 3.3. Every organization should have a well-defined cost chain of command.

The ACE staff shadow organization provides each subordinate manager with his own analytic cost expert (Figure 3.4). The parallel organization also provides a strong quality control function on that expertise by making each expert part of the overall control function.

Furthermore, the shadow organization provides the chief executive with an obvious lever of control to quickly execute financial management directives while continuously working issues of financial management policy.

An institutionalized managerial coster staff of ACEs may offer the further advantage of continuity. When managers move, the ACE keeps the control process running. Having an experienced manager in place as well as the hierarchy of the shadow organization moderates a situation in which the ACE moves.

ACE Staff Responsibilities

ACE responsibilities lie at the interface of management action, the review process, and cost information (Figure 3.5). The ACE has significant responsibilities in linking all three elements. Essentially, the control staff becomes the owner of the numbers and the enabler of the leadership driven cost management and control process.

ACE Staff Shadow Organization

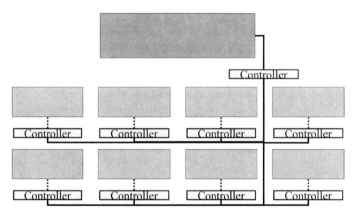

Figure 3.4. The analytic cost expert staff of managerial costers also has a hierarchy that parallels the cost chain of command.

ACE Staff Responsibilities

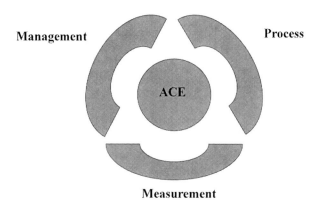

Figure 3.5. The ACE managerial costing staff is at the center of management, review process, and measurement. They hold it all together.

The managerial coster has distinct responsibilities for each segment of the control process.

ACE Staff Responsibilities Related to Management

The ACE should be the "right arm" of the operational leader/manager. As mentioned earlier, managers in government typically do not have a strong financial control background. Managers must be able to depend on their ACE to help the manager meet his or her accountability obligations and drive continuous improvement.

The ACE should develop a trusted advisor relationship with the operational manager. The ACE will often be speaking for the boss on financial management issues and must be sensitive to those implications. The ACE will also be the eyes and ears of the boss regarding problems and potential problems within the organization.

Accomplishing these objectives requires that the ACE be part of the manager's team; for example, attending staff and other routine management meetings. Duties also include public and private briefings to the boss on financial status as well as the overall control process (Figure 3.6).

ACE Relationships to Leadership and Process

Figure 3.6. The analytic cost expert supports and enables the reviews given to and by his operating boss.

These briefings provide the opportunity for the ACE to educate management about financial issues and to offer advice on alternative management actions. This often includes, for example, suggesting questions the manager might ask or issues the manager might raise at the periodic review.

ACE Staff Responsibilities Related to Process

The ACE owns the cost estimating and cost review processes. ACE responsibilities include scheduling the reviews, organizing the agenda, and defining the requirements for details of required presentations. Of course, the operational manager to whom the ACE reports officially schedules the meeting. That manager, however, should rely on the ACE to make it happen.

ACE Staff Responsibilities Related to Cost Measurement

Finally, the ACE has significant responsibilities for cost and, perhaps, even performance accounting. The ACE should be the "keeper of the numbers." As such, he or she has primary responsibilities for quality assurance. Cost accounting credibility should be constantly maintained and diligently guarded. All questions about accuracy should be quickly investigated. Most will result in educating the questioner regarding the source of the cost. Some, however, will uncover measurement anomalies that must be addressed. Either outcome yields increased credibility and management confidence in the numbers.

The managerial coster should be the preferred source for cost related questions from the management team. This often means that efforts and abilities will be directed to ad hoc studies and analyses on a wide range of operational issues. The ACE must be closely integrated into the organization. It is not sufficient to answer a "what does it cost" question with a number. The ACE must understand why the question has been asked and the context of the question. Only then can the proper answer be constructed to provide the right view of cost using the costing techniques and assumptions that provide the most useful answer.

Developing the ACE Managerial Costing Staff

Developing an effective managerial costing staff requires identification or recruitment of people with the right skill set. Training and capability building are also required.

Finding the right people in a government organization is especially problematic because most existing accounting staffers are probably skilled in financial accounting rather than managerial accounting, and the two skills may be mutually exclusive to an important degree.

Financial accounting people typically deal with compliance to external reporting requirements. This requires knowledge of generally accepted accounting procedures and all relevant rules and requirements because audits are normally expected of such reporting. Little procedural latitude is allowed. Assumptions and analysis are not typical. This profession deals with fact, and the output of the process is a set of procedurally compliant numbers.

Managerial costing requires a different skill set. Compliance is less an issue because much of the work is unique, and consistency to other organizations is less important. Assumptions and analysis are common. Judgment is frequently required and common sense valued. The set of numbers the financial accountant provides represents raw materials to the managerial coster who then seek to build managerially useful views of cost or informative analyses to address specific issues of importance.

People seem to self-select into either external reporting or managerial coster arenas. It may be that the personalities that excel in each area are mutually exclusive. External reporting oriented people may be uncomfortable with the greater degree of ambiguity and judgment required in ACE positions. Managerial costing oriented people may not like the detailed compliance driven requirements of external reporting.

Surprisingly, good managerial costing skills are often found in people without much formal accounting training. Perhaps this should not be surprising because most formal accounting education is dedicated to external reporting. People who excel at and enjoy the challenge and ambiguity of managerial costing might well have found other courses and majors more interesting.

Conclusions

The ACE staff of managerial costers has a critically important role to play in cost management and control. They are the key financial advisors to operating management. They organize and run the process of reviews and meetings. They provide the credible cost insights and information required by management and process.

The existing capabilities of most government organizations in this area are arguably extremely weak. Thus the development of the ACE staff is the most critical need in organizations beginning the transformation to leadership driven management.

The chief executive who seeks leadership driven management's benefits must first develop a strong staff of ACEs and then, using this staff as a tool to educate and develop subordinates, evolve the control process, and define and refine management information requirements.

CHAPTER 4

Army Central Command Examples of Cost Benefit Analysis

When military actions were initiated in Iraq and Afghanistan, it was assumed they would not be long-lived actions. Consequently, they were viewed as contingencies and funded by supplemental appropriations.

The United States Central Command (USCENTCOM) directs these military actions. Army Central Command (ARCENT) is the U.S. Army component of USCENTCOM. According to its website,[1] its mission is as follows:

- Provides support and services to theater ARFOR [Army Forces] commands, as well as directed Army support to other services
- Conducts Theater Security Cooperation activities
- Provides a forward based service component command to plan and, on order, conduct land operations across the USCENT-COM area of responsibility
- Supports force rotations; conducts reception, staging, and onward movement; and provides theater sustainment and other support as required to forces in Iraq, Afghanistan, and the Horn of Africa

War fighters were not budgeted. Their "requirements" were met by a wealthy and angry nation. The economic downturn may be responsible for increased emphasis on cost informed decision making.

Mandate for Change

Brigadier General Phillip McGhee arrived as ARCENT Director of Resource Management in the fall of 2008 with a mandate from the Honorable Nelson Ford, Army Under Secretary, to "bring a cost culture to Theater." The difficulty of this task was significant. Cost competency has never been included in the training, development, or selection of officers. Moreover, as one senior commander stated, "We have unfortunately 'trained' a generation of young officers to think that resources are unlimited." Even some senior leaders at the time bristled at the idea that anything besides military effectiveness was their responsibility.

The message from the Under Secretary was not an isolated event. Senior leaders had begun hearing the same thing from their chain of command. Army Chief of Staff General George Casey had concluded that better cost management was critical to maintaining Army effectiveness given the national economy, political imperatives for withdrawal, and shifting national assets to nondefense spending. Consider memos from General David Petraeus, USCENTCOM Commanding General, and from General Casey and Army Secretary Peter Geren (see Figures 4.7 and 4.8).

These events and situations resulted in the call for a cost culture:

The U.S. Army Central (ARCENT) and Coalition Forces Land Component Command (CFLCC) Commanding General, Lieutenant General James Lovelace tasked his Resource Manager, Brigadier General Phillip McGhee, to foster a cost culture within the command throughout Southwest Asia to ensure leaders at all echelons consider cost relative to effects in their decision making processes.[2]

Embedded Assets

Brigadier General McGhee found an environment receptive to change and new ideas. Lieutenant General James J. Lovelace, ARCENT Commanding General, approved a multidimensioned strategy for improvement that included developing the organization's cost culture. One of Brigadier General McGhee's first actions was to request deployment of "costers," perhaps the first time costers were sent to an active theater of war. Deputy

Assistant Secretary for Cost and Economics Stephen Bagby responded by sending Mort Anvari, one of his most experienced and capable cost estimators, and a team of 12 contractors.

Perhaps more important, Brigadier General McGhee resisted the temptation to keep this staff as a headquarters unit to critique or to audit supported units. Instead, he "embedded" most of the team in field and subordinate commands with the mandate to support their assigned organization. In this role, costers rarely took positions on decision alternatives. Instead, they concentrated on providing unbiased, credible cost estimates, useful to commanders in making decisions. Supported commanders soon recognized that they now had a valuable "intelligence" asset in executing General Petraeus's wishes concerning improved stewardship.

CARBs and Science Projects

Costers were quickly brought into the Coalition Acquisition Review Board (CARB) process. Their role was to review, make cost estimates, or both, especially considering alternatives to proposed acquisition plans. "Science projects," however, were directed analyses or models aimed at addressing specific issues. Both types of studies involved making studied estimates of future costs as part of decision making. The ARCENT paper titled "Theater Strategic Financial Management Initiatives" describes the situation as follows:

> Commanders value the need to manage costs when conducting their missions but possess limited capabilities, resources, and required skill sets to perform detailed cost analyses of capability gaps. Eight years of persistent conflict resulted in a consumption-based approach that focuses on mission accomplishment without adequately addressing more efficient capability alternatives . . .
>
> Products will provide commanders with a better understanding of their full capability cost and promote the incorporation of cost considerations into the decision-making cycle. This approach will allow commanders to understand the near and long-term cost implications of their decisions and make effective trade-off decisions to achieve best use of limited resources. (p. 10)

The cost team studied the relationships between requirements, capacity, and the cost of capacity. The team discovered two things: first, a diminishing return to cost at high levels of capacity and, second, that support infrastructure and capacity had not downsized as combat resources were withdrawn from the theater (see Figures 4.1 and 4.2). This resulted in unneeded costs for excess capacities.

> ARCENT continues to work to determine the right level of readiness at the right level of industrial capacity, at the right cost, while maximizing effectiveness and efficiency between JOAs. We continue to better understand why it cost what it cost in theater to conduct Counter Insurgency (COIN) operations so that commanders make informed resource decisions. ARCENT has captured theater cost drivers and then developed a model that accurately described the relationship among requirements, readiness, industrial capacity, and cost. The cost analysis team created the Readiness, Requirements, Capacity and Cost (R2C2) model by using fiscal year 2008 expenditure data as the R2C2 baseline. ARCENT continues to refine this model as each cost area impacting industrial capacity is examined Units, Stocks, Equipment,

Relationship Between Requirements and Capacity (Cost)

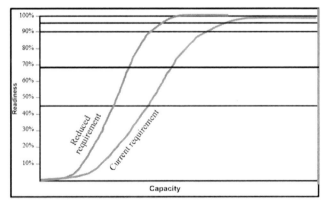

Figure 4.1. Analysis showed diminishing return to capacity at high readiness levels and the impact of reduced readiness requirements.

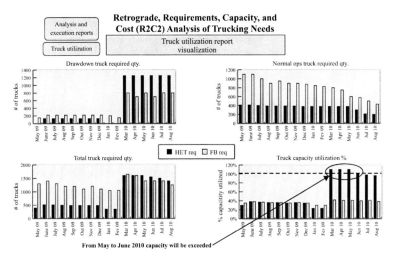

Figure 4.2. Analysis of truck requirements during upcoming withdrawal from Iraq showed that needs would exceed capability: allowing time for corrective action.

Contractors, and the Logistics Civil Augmentation Program (LOGCAP). The next step is to provide a process and structure to estimate future theater resource requirements. These two efforts are optimizing readiness and allowing the Commander of ARCENT to reduce in theater industrial capacity and cost. (p. 6)

Container Refurbishment "No Brainer"

The impending withdrawal from Iraq caused planners to note that many of the 90,000 truck-sized shipping containers in country were not in good shape to be accepted aboard ship. This observation resulted in a request to refurbish thousands of containers at a cost of millions of dollars.

Cost analysis of this request started with a review of the number of containers actually needed to accomplish the mission. It was determined that only 8,000 containers were required to meet all shipping needs. The number of containers already qualified for sea shipment exceeded this requirement:

Cost to refurbish all containers	$ xxM
Benefit to refurbish all containers	$ 0M

Plans and contracts for container refurbishment were dropped, as there was obviously no benefit to incurring costs to refurbish containers that would be left in Iraq (Figure 4.3). The technical accounting term for this obvious cost informed decision is "no brainer."

Main Battle Tank Requirements

A costing effort (affectionately labeled a science project) that spun out of the retrograde analysis involved the main battle tanks based in Iraq. Main battle tanks had not been used much in their intended roles since the initial invasion. The changing nature of the conflict now favored mine-resistant, ambush-protected vehicles.

Undoubtedly, there is a benefit to having a significant armored force in Iraq. That benefit, however, is probably based on contingencies, that is, "what-ifs." For example, "What if Iran invaded?" Or, "What if some other regional conflict brewed into a high-intensity conflict that needed overwhelming armor capabilities?" Quantifying this benefit is highly subjective and entirely assumption based.

On the other hand, it is relatively easy to quantify many of the costs of keeping this force in Iraq. The cost team evaluated sustainment, fuel, transport, repair, and arms costs for the force and its soldiers. However, it is likely that other relevant costs may be hard, if not impossible, to quantify (Figure 4.4). For example, armor training in the continental United States may suffer because of the lack of machine availability. It is also possible that there is some "cost" in not having this force in other areas in the world (e.g., South Korea).

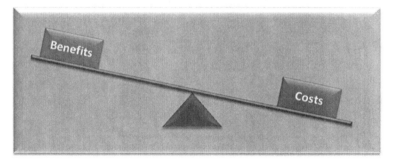

Figure 4.3. Costs to refurbish 8,000 containers provided no benefit.

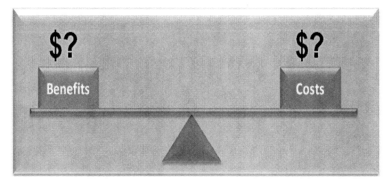

Figure 4.4. Many of the costs of keeping a large armor force in Iraq can be estimated. However, the benefits and some of the costs are unquantifiable.

Who should make these judgments and weigh the results? Clearly, not the cost estimator. The cost estimator provides a credible estimate based on clearly stated assumptions and conditions. The chain of command should use this "intelligence" like any other to make policy.

Geopolitical Impact of Shipping Route: Thinking Outside the Box

As mentioned earlier, some 8,000 containers will be shipped from the Iraq theater coincident with withdrawal. Early plans assumed Kuwait as the port of departure. General Petraeus, however, believed that significant benefit would accrue in the alliance with Jordan if substantial shipments were made through that country.

Costers estimated the costs per container from two Iraqi cities through both alternatives. They performed this analysis with three different data sources, as shown in Figure 4.5.

On average, cost estimators showed that it cost an additional $2,060 per container to ship via Jordan, some 22.6% more. If all 8,000 containers paid this extra tariff, the incremental cost totaled roughly $16.5 million. The value of the "benefit" to Jordanian relations, however, is unquantifiable (Figure 4.6). It could also be argued that the "cost" to Kuwaiti relations is also unquantifiable. General Petraeus faced the following decision:

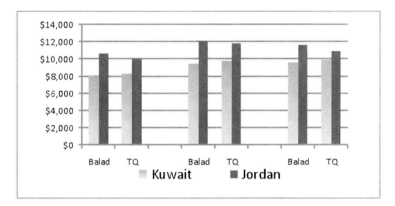

Figure 4.5. Three cost estimates were made from two locations in
Iraq (Balad and TQ) comparing shipping costs to the United States
via Kuwait and via Jordan.

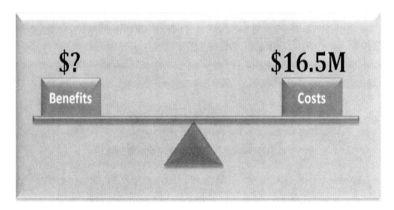

Figure 4.6. Shipping costs via Jordan were fairly definitive, but the
costs and benefits of the geopolitical relationship were unquantifiable.

Having recently issued instructions (Figure 4.7) emphasizing cost
stewardship, General Petraeus used the cost "intelligence" he received to
expand his alternatives:

1. Send all containers through Jordan and accept the extra cost of
   $16.5 million.
2. Send some fraction of the 8,000 containers through Jordan and
   accept that fraction of the $16.5 million additional cost.

3. Negotiate with Jordan for lower rates per container and try to create a "win-win" situation in which both parties achieve benefits and without incurring additional cost to the United States.

At last input, General Petraeus was preparing to show cost estimates to King Abdullah, and both Jordanian and Kuwaiti shippers were looking for ways to lower their bids.

UNCLASSIFIED

From: CDR USCENTCOM PERSONAL FOR

To: CDR, MNF-I; CDR, USFOR-A; CDR, ARCENT; CDR, NAVCENT; CDR, AFCENT; CDR,
MARCENT;CDR,SOCCENT

Info: VCJCS, DEPSECDEF

Precedence: PRIORITY

Classification: UNCLASSIFIED

Subject: FISCAL RESPONSIBILITY

COMMANDERS, AS OUR NATION AND ITS INSTITUTIONS COME TOGETHER TO SEE THE COUNTRY THROUGH A DEEPENING GLOBAL ECONOMIC CRISIS, I BELIEVE IT FALLS TO ALL OF US TO DO OUR PART. THROUGHOUT OPERATIONS ENDURING FREEDOM AND IRAQI FREEDOM, THE ADMINISTRATION AND CONGRESS HAVE SHOWN CONSISTENTLY STRONG SUPPORT FOR U.S. CENTRAL COMMAND'S RESOURCE REQUIREMENTS. WE HAVE, IN TURN, WORKED PARTICULARLY HARD TO DEMONSTRATE OUR GOOD STEWARDSHIP OF THE RESOURCES PROVIDED. NONETHELESS, WE MUST EACH REDOUBLE OUR EFFORTS IN THAT REGARD. WE MUST ENSURE THE AUTHORITIES AND FUNDING MADE AVAILABLE TO US ARE USED MOST EFFECTIVELY AND EFFICIENTLY TO MEET OUR HIGHEST PRIORITIES, AND IAW THE PURPOSES FOR WHICH THEY WERE GIVEN. WHEN NEW REQUIREMENTS COME TO THE FORE, I URGE YOU TO EMPLOY YOUR FISCAL, LEGAL, AND CONTRACTING EXPERTS EARLY IN DEVELOPING OR REQUESTING PROPER AND RESPONSIVE RESOURCE SOLUTIONS. FOR THE ASSETS YOU ALREADY CONTROL OR WILL RECEIVE, PLEASE STRESS TO LEADERS AT ALL LEVELS THE IMPORTANCE OF GOOD MANAGEMENT CONTROLS, SOUND ACQUISITION STRATEGIES, AND THE ABILITY TO MEASURE EFFECTIVE PERFORMANCE DURING EXECUTION. I APPLAUD YOUR PAST EFFORTS AND ASK YOU TO CONVEY THROUGHOUT YOUR CHAIN OF COMMAND THE NEED FOR COMMON SENSE AND CONSCIENTIOUS STEWARDSHIP OF RESOURCES AS WE UNDERTAKE THE CHALLENGING TASKS AHEAD.

SINCERELY,

GEN PETRAEUS

Figure 4.7. General Petraeus's memo.

DEPARTMENT OF THE ARMY
WASHINGTON DC 20310-0200

15 JAN 2009

MEMORANDUM FOR SEE DISTRIBUTION

SUBJECT: Institutional Adaptation and Army Transformation

1. The Army has made a deliberate effort, over time, to improve how it functions as an organization. Secretary White and General Shinseki provided the intellectual framework for the 21st Century Army and initiated our transformation from a Cold War Army to a campaign quality expeditionary force, capable of meeting the needs of the combatant commanders across the spectrum of conflict. Secretary Harvey and General Schoomaker led the next phase, focusing on modularity and organizational change. We will continue our transformation by adapting our institutions to support an Army on a rotational cycle in an era of persistent conflict. We will not cement the hard-won changes of the past decade until this occurs.

2. There are three major elements to Institutional Adaptation. First, the Army will improve how we execute ARFORGEN by revising the model for institutional support of the ARFORGEN process. Second, the Army will adopt an enterprise approach, by developing an Army-wide strategic management system that incorporates a refined governance process supported by an improved assessment architecture. Third, the Army will reform its requirements and resource processes by establishing a more responsive and realistic requirements process and indicating a cost culture that incentivizes good stewardship. The confluence of these three efforts is designed to improve both the effectiveness and efficiency of the Army and align our institutions to support the Army of the 21st Century and preserve our All Volunteer Force.

3. The ability to manage as an enterprise is critical to restoring balance. The Army will establish the Army Enterprise Board (AEB), with representation from the Secretariat and Army Commands, that meets routinely. The AEB will review strategic Army issues and recommend solutions to the Secretary of the Army. The board will supervise our functional alignment into core enterprises in accordance with Title 10, General Orders No. 3, and Army Regulations on a schedule that will not impact current operations. The AEB Charter and the implementing instructions will be developed and published over the course of this year with a goal of IOC of March 2009 and FOC of August 2009.

4. Institutional Adaptation is the final and essential element of our transformation from a Cold War force to an agile, disciplined warrior team that is dominant across the spectrum of 21st Century conflict. We need your full support.

George W. Casey, Jr.
General, United States Army
Chief of Staff

Pete Geren
Secretary of the Army

Figure 4.8. Memos from the Secretary of the Army and the Chief of Staff.

Conclusions

These three scenarios describe typical cost benefit analysis scenarios. The container refurbishment decision ended up with a very clear-cut result. In the process of validating the costs, costers thought to check on the requirements. This resulted in a very easy decision that was decisive and obviously correct.

The main battle tank issue is just the opposite. It is impossible to evaluate definitively the benefits of main battle tanks in the theater. Some of the costs can be estimated, but not all of them can be definitively posted.

Decisions of this nature can be influenced by cost estimates but ultimately rely on the informed judgment of the leader in charge.

The issue of shipping containers through Jordan displays another common result. Looking at costs stimulates thinking about alternatives. In many situations, cost is not some absolute number. Rather, it is a variable based on some technique. Even though the costers built their conclusions on the basis of three different estimates, "cost" to the Army is a "price" to the shipper. Prices are often negotiable.

PART II

Stage II Cost Use

Creating Cost Managed Organizations

Making cost informed decisions is a good thing: But it is just scratching the surface in unlocking the value of cost use in leadership driven management. (See Figure 5.1.) Cost Managed Organizations (CMOs) make hundreds of cost informed decisions. Furthermore, they expand the venue from ad hoc use to an institutionalized process of systematically looking at costs and cost stimulated innovation.

Cost benefit analysis, by its nature as a decision making tool, provides valuable guidance in making good plans. Something more is needed,

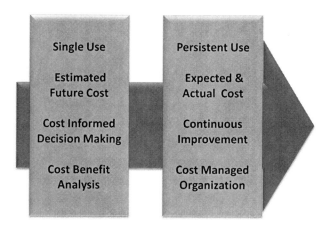

Figure 5.1. While cost informed decision making uses cost benefit analysis to make superior decisions, it takes a cost managed organization to ensure performance. Cost managed organizations expand the role of cost use as part of their continuous improvement process.

however, to reap the benefits assumed in the cost benefit analysis. That something is a cost management process as part of a Cost Managed Organization.

We have previously described the use of cost intelligence in making cost informed decisions in which a cost benefit tradeoff is required. Remember the example of the lion's cost benefit tradeoffs in deciding what prey to hunt. Rabbits and elephants fail the cost benefit calculus, while gazelles seemingly fit the bill. It seems that the lion is ideally adapted and evolved to hunt the gazelle.

However, simply making the right prey decision does not guarantee a successful hunt. Good cost benefit decision making leads the lion to hunt gazelle rather than rabbits or elephants. However, that good decision does not mean the lion actually catches the gazelle automatically. A successful hunt requires good execution. The hunt must be executed with precision, power, cunning, and stealth. Success is far from guaranteed.[1]

CMOs are concerned with execution. Likewise, lions that live to maturity have learned a lot from their successes and maybe more from their failures as they master their "business."

CMOs represent an expanded role of cost information utilization. While cost informed decision making uses estimates of future costs, CMOs require actual cost information and some form of expected costs. Actual costs impose a new enabling requirement, cost measurement, which will be further discussed in chapter 6. Expected costs can come from a formal or informal plan or from something as simple as previous actual cost trends.

The second new enabling requirement is a cost management process (chapter 5). Differences or variances are exposed during the process of comparing actual cost to expected cost. This comparison triggers efficient learning as leaders focus on the larger variances. This approach is called *management by exception*. Significant differences beg for answers about why things went worse than expected and what improvements can be made or for answers about why things went better than expected and what can be done permanently to capture that result or to expand its impact.

Explaining the differences is a management responsibility. Telling the story inevitably requires some research and learning. The CMO process capitalizes on that learning by seeking improvement in operational execution or perhaps even refined expectation generation or actual cost measurement.

The CMO process inevitably creates a public meeting or forum. This forum offers an opportunity for leadership to teach and participants to learn. Presenters tell their story about their operations' performance during the time period of record. They are expected to be able to coherently explain "their" costs and to offer solutions to problems and suggest improvements to operations based on their learning.

Observed Types of CMOs in Government

CMOs are rare in government. However, a number have been observed that could serve as models for larger efforts to improve cost effectiveness in government.

The observed successes exhibit many differences. However, it does seem possible to group them into three categories. Organization based processes seem to use the naturally occurring accountability relationships found in the organization chart. Fort Huachuca typifies this type of successful control process. This case study is presented in chapter 8.

The SPAWAR Systems Center Pacific, however, relied on role relationships between line and support functions to build a control function that increased the cost effectiveness of overhead functions in their role of supporting the line, direct mission function. (See chapter 10.)

The Bureau of Engraving and Printing case study typifies the possibilities for a government organization with well-defined outputs. In this case, the cost control process is built around the output: currency printing. This case study is presented in chapter 12.

A number of similarities can be generalized. First, and most important, is that these processes are leadership driven. They are not accounting exercises. They all have the other three requirements previously listed: (a) a cost management process with a formal after action review meeting, (b) a strong staff that supports the accountable manager/leaders, and (c) cost measurement processes tailored to the needs of the process.

The selected examples for case studies all have one other very important attribute: *they have stood the test of time*. Many management books and case studies describe "successes" that, unfortunately, do not persist. The case studies here have worked long enough not to be "fads"

Table 5.1. Summary of Cases

	Organization Based Control	Role Based Control	Output Based Control
Example	Fort Huachuca Garrison	SPAWAR Systems Center Pacific	Bureau of Engraving and Printing
Savings	Redirected Internally	Lower Stabilized Rate (Fee)	Lower User Fee Price
Frequency	Quarterly	Monthly	Monthly
Presenter	Subordinate	Overhead Manager	Manufacturing
Principals	Garrison Commander	Managers of Line Organizations	Bureau Director
Audience	Subordinate Peers	Overhead Manager's Peers	All Executives
Years of Experience	10	15	20

or dependent on a single, visionary leader. The Fort Huachuca process worked well for 10 years, the SPAWAR Systems Center Pacific process has been in existence for 15 years, and the Bureau of Engraving's process has evolved over the past 20 years.

Much can be learned from these organizations.

CHAPTER 5

Constructing Interactive, Learning Oriented Processes

Differentiating Leadership and Rule Driven Control Processes

Cost informed decision making is an act. Cost management is a process. The reason for the distinction is that cost management occurs through people, a natural venue for leadership. The process provides leaders the forum to drive management. It gives them the opportunity to signal, direct, influence, and teach.

Leadership driven control processes differ significantly from the rule driven control processes typical of government oversight functions. Rules provide boundaries and restraints to behavior. They preserve the status quo by telling people what they are not allowed to do. They also tell people exactly what they are supposed to do.

Bob Stone, a former Deputy Assistant Secretary of Defense for Installations, offered the following commentary on rules: "My guess is that a third of the defense budget goes into the friction of following bad regulations—doing work that doesn't have to be done."[2] He noted that many rules often prohibited one from doing what should be done, and other rules required people to do things that really did not need to be done. Stone also provided many examples of the inefficiency of trying to manage within a paradigm of rules, regulations, and restrictions.

He also showed the creativity of people in getting around the rules. For example, soldiers in hot climates discovered that putting a hot light bulb near the thermostat could trick the air conditioning into cooling the room effectively while not violating the rule about thermostat settings. Simply lowering the thermostat to the desired setting would have saved the energy used to burn the light bulb and then to remove its heat from the room.

Operating solely under a management paradigm of rules, regulations, and restrictions is silly. Rules, of course, serve a valuable function in creating boundaries. They do not make sense when they try to govern all behavior and substitute for common sense and good judgment.

Leadership driven management control processes seek to motivate people to do those things that should be done and not to do those that do not need to be done. Accomplishing this goal requires a new financial management operating paradigm. The overall goal is "how can we operate to improve mission effectiveness by using resources more efficiently."

Determining the "Right" Action to Pursue

"Knowing" the right things to do is often not obvious. The right thing to do is often changing dynamically. The right thing to do is also often different in one part of an organization. Centralized, rule driven processes cannot cope with diverse, fast-changing environments. The efficiency of rule driven paradigms probably decreases as organizations get larger and more complex.

This brings us to the realm of centralization versus decentralization. Without getting into a theoretical discussion, suffice it to say that there are tradeoffs. The goal here is to suggest that subordinate organizations are fully capable of making good resource decisions better than those coming from a rule driven paradigm. Doing so requires an operational process that drives continuous improvement while adhering to the overall goals and directions of the greater entity.

The Addition of Leadership Driven Management Control

It would not make sense to throw out all the rules. The goal is to improve operational performance by energizing learning and continuous improvement. Inevitably, this practice should reduce reliance on rule driven processes but is unlikely to eliminate them.

Leadership driven management processes provide an additive control that may be the primary operational control mechanism at lower levels of the organization. The process institutionalizes a structured, periodic, disciplined mechanism that ensures timely interaction on financial performance and process improvement issues. Leadership driven management control creates an environment that can use the capabilities and creativity of the governmental workforce to accomplish their organizations' missions more cost effectively.

Because there is no rule book that merely seeks simple compliance, organizations must intelligently search for the ever better way to operate. Two questions are keys to stimulating the learning required in this process:

1. How did you perform relative to your expectation?
2. What are you doing to improve?

Performance Improvement Requirement

Leadership driven management control requires managers, supervisors, and employees at all levels of the organization to explain their performance. Many career managers and employees have never had to do this under the current, rule driven paradigm.

The results of requiring performance explanation are often startling because accountable managers must research mission accomplishment and resource consumption issues to fulfill the requirement. Inevitably, learning occurs, and this learning is the underlying goal of asking the performance question.

Current practice exempts many long-term career employees from this research and learning. As long as their budget officer verified that spending rates did not risk Anti-Deficiency Act violation, managers did not need to get involved in the details of their operations.

The performance explanation requirement changes this current, benign operational environment. Lack of knowledge and understanding is quickly exposed. Most managers quickly come down the learning curve and are soon much more attuned to their performance output and resource utilization. This knowledge works hand in hand with the second key requirement embedded in the "improvement" question.

Improvement Explanation Requirement

Understanding performance is a prerequisite to improving performance. Answering the "improvement" question requires managers to change their focus and to be proactively and aggressively thinking about change. Again, this kind of thinking is not necessary in the rule driven management paradigm. Avoiding improvement forgoes tremendous opportunity and over time results in acceptance of very inefficient operating practices.

Most government employees seem to welcome the opportunity to fix inefficient practices and policies. They often express that they would not run their households or business interests the way the Federal Government does. They also tend to believe strongly in the missions of their organizations and like to see their improvement ideas translated into better operations.

Goal Setting

Setting goals for performance and improvement adds a very powerful lever to the leadership driven management control process. Setting goals also injects greater levels of accountability into the organization culture. Goals provide targets for improvement that are never achieved with the paradigm of rules, regulations, and restrictions.

The key cultural dimension is the creation of expectations. Personnel will respond to the organizational norm of expectations for more efficient performance and the generation of continuous improvement initiatives.

Performance expectations also provide a basis for comparison that sharpens the management review process. Some organizations might build strong performance expectations by generating forecasts, short-term budgets, standards, or projections. Others might simply use prior performance, particularly at the start of their process development. In either case, current results can be compared with an expectation based on projected commitments or previous period performance.

This comparison focuses management attention by enabling management by exception. Generally, most elements of performance meet expectations. These usually do not need much management attention. Relatively more management attention, however, is needed in the areas that significantly exceeded expectations or significantly fell short of expectations. The leadership driven management control process should concentrate effort in these areas.

Setting goals for continuous improvement initiatives tends to motivate their generation. Goals can be in the number, the value of such improvements, or both. Savings can be costed with some accuracy, but spending too much effort on evaluation can be costly as well as potentially demotivating. Many good improvements are difficult to evaluate, particularly if they involve cost avoidances or quality improvements.

The Basic Leadership Driven Control Process

Creating expectations is the first step of a four-step control cycle:

1. Form Expectations.
2. Execute Operations.
3. Measure Results.
4. Conduct After Action Review.

The role of planning is to create expectations for execution. Measurement defines what actually happened. The after action review compares measured performance with planned performance and provides a forum to explain performance and, it is hoped, to learn things that impact the next planning, execution, and measurement steps. (See Figure 5.2.)

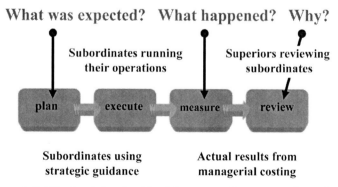

The Basic Control Process

What was expected?   What happened?   Why?

Subordinates running their operations

Superiors reviewing subordinates

plan   execute   measure   review

Subordinates using strategic guidance

Actual results from managerial costing

Figure 5.2. The basic leadership driven control process asks and answers three key questions.

Forming Expectations for Performance and Improvement

The operations cycle starts with expectation forming. Even when a formal planning effort does not occur, expectation forming is implicitly occurring. In that case, planning is simply continuing past practice, and prior period performance can be considered the plan or expectation for future performance.

Creating expectations is what planning is about. Planning creates a specific benchmark to be compared against actual performance when the period of execution is over. More sophisticated planning starts with prior performance and adjusts planned future performance for known changes or projected improvements. One goal of a control process is "no surprises." Good planning helps ensure this goal is met.

In any case, planned performance expectations can be thought of as creating the front end of an accountability loop. The plan represents a performance commitment. The manager responsible for the plan assumes complete and full responsibility for its accomplishment, so plans are not something to take lightly and often involve negotiations. The manager responsible for execution typically seeks less challenging planned commitments while higher level management typically seeks more aggressive challenging plans.

Challenging plans are an important technique in bringing out the best in an organization. However, challenging plans are more likely to not be achieved. This creates an interesting problem: motivating component organizations to stretch performance while avoiding "surprises" inherent in missing planned commitments.

A commonly used technique is to incorporate a "judgment" entity into the organizational consolidation stream. As shown in Table 5.2, this judgment entity adds to the consolidation of subordinate organizations. "Right way" judgment makes the consolidation more conservative and more likely to be achieved. "Wrong way" judgment has the opposite effect and is usually used only temporarily to reflect a top down goal quickly before it is passed to lower levels.

Consider the following scenario. Initially, the consolidated organization has a $300 spending plan that is fully reflected in the subordinate organizations.

Table 5.2. First Scenario

	Component Orgs				Consolidated Org
	A	B	C	Judgment	
Spending Plan	100	100	100	0	300

Next, imagine a $20 performance goal imposed on the consolidated organization by a higher authority. Initially, wrong way judgment might be taken so that the consolidated organization reflects the wishes of higher authority, and its plans can be further consolidated to higher levels. The following matrix reflects this wrong way judgment (see Table 5.3).

Achieving the $20 spending reduction is unlikely to occur unless Components A, B, and C are actively working on plans to make it happen. The consolidated organization manager would be wise to push the goal to component managers. However, the consolidation manager might wish to overplan the reduction to minimize the risk of missing the consolidated organization plan. The following matrix shows assignment of a $10 spending reduction to each component that now permits $10 of right way judgment (see Table 5.4).

These techniques can work similarly for other things that management wishes to control. For example, they might be used to plan headcount or even the number of continuous improvement initiatives. Continuous improvement plans might be based on the number of initiatives, the value of initiatives, or both. The key is that planning requires managers to think ahead and to assume responsibility for the future. This encourages

Table 5.3. Second Scenario

	Component Orgs				Consolidated Org
	A	B	C	Judgment	
Spending Plan	100	100	100	−20	280

Table 5.4. Third Scenario

	Component Orgs				Consolidated Org
	A	B	C	Judgment	
Spending Plan	90	90	90	10	280

a more aggressive, forward leaning culture that is more likely to achieve progress than one that merely waits passively for things to happen.

Execute Operations

The control process shown in Figure 5.1 is basic. It works for most, if not all, types of operations. The length of the time period of execution before measurement and after action review will vary based on leadership's needs.

Some dynamic or critically important operations may desire periods of execution as short as daily or weekly. Manufacturing operations may wish monthly or weekly cycles. Operations that are primarily service oriented may be able to operate effectively with quarterly control cycles.

Some organizations start with more frequent cycles to move down the learning curve more rapidly. After 6 to 12 monthly cycles, they may move to quarterly or decide that monthly reviews are more appropriate. This decision should be based on a comparison of costs and benefits of less frequent reviews.

There is some added effort and cost to more frequent cycles. There are also benefits from the process that may diminish if the process is too infrequent. Quarterly or semiannual cycles may fail to keep people engaged and can evolve into periodic exercises rather than being a critical part of the organization culture.

Measurement

Once the period of execution has ended, it is prudent to take stock. The goal of the measurement process is to establish objective facts. What were the outputs? What was the cost? What improvement initiatives were developed?

These questions can all be answered objectively. The measurement process simply seeks to understand the truth. Measurement issues are important. They will be discussed separately in chapter 6. An impartial third party often creates managerially useful information from the measurement. That third party is the analytic cost expert support staff discussed previously in chapter 3.

The After Action Review

The after action review is perhaps the most important aspect of the leadership driven management control process. Some organizations call this a debriefing, some in the Army would recognize it as a Quarterly Training Brief, and some in the Navy call it a "Hot Wash." In all cases, this review represents a formal comparison of accomplishment to expectation. (See Figure 5.3.)

It is here that expected performance is compared with measured performance. Most important, this review is not a report. It is an engagement of key people with the goal of learning things that will facilitate accomplishing the organization's missions.

The key requirement is that subordinate managers personally present answers to the two key questions involving achieved performance and improvement ideas. Comparison to planned levels facilitates and focuses discussion.

Action items for future action should result, including better plans, better execution, and better measurement in future cycles. Good performance should be recognized and actions taken to improve poor performance.

The Learning Process

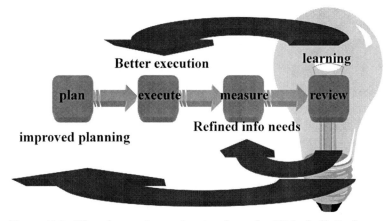

Figure 5.3. The after action review is where the "light bulbs" of discovery should burn brightest.

After Action Reconciliation

	Case A	Case B
Spending		
What was Expected	$X	$X
What was Achieved	$X – $20	$X + $20
Delta	$20	($20)
Reconciliation Format		
Good News Story	$	$
Good News Story	$	$
Bad News Story	($)	($)
Bad News Story	($)	($)
Total Explained	$20	($20)

Figure 5.4. The template shows a favorable and unfavorable case and a simple format to tell the stories behind the performance.

Answering the "what happened" question can be sharpened by using a standard reconciliation template. Figure 5.4 shows a simple format for two cases. In Case A, the organization has spent $20 less than planned. This is good and is considered as a favorable delta, or variance. Telling the story cites the handful of reasons explaining that variance. Each reason has a dollar value that totals to the delta that must be explained. Case B shows as organization that overspent its plan by $20. This is shown as ($20), with the brackets indicating that this variance is unfavorable. In Case B, explanatory reasons must add up to the ($20).

Winning the Cost War[3] provides details on experiences with the steps in the control process. This book notes that the military's command and control processes for battlefield management provide useful techniques for government organizations seeking financial management and control. Battlefield commanders are inherently cost managers, as they seek mission accomplishment with the fewest possible casualties. They seek to learn from their experiences and to improve their skills continuously. Financial managers in government can learn much from this process, regardless of their missions.

Conclusions

Most of what the press labels as accounting problems in government are really accountability problems. The leadership driven control process enhances accountability by institutionalizing periodic reviews of accomplishment compared with expectation. Such a process of frequent review is a powerful technique to detect and correct small problems before they become big problems worthy of press coverage.

The leadership driven management control process is very different from the budget control process. Currently used management control processes typically rely on rules, regulations, and restrictions. For example, the budget control process relies heavily on the Anti-Deficiency Act and its criminal penalties for noncompliance to achieve its success.

While rules provide good boundaries, they are not very useful for making all the decisions that must be made in large, complex organizations. Furthermore, rule based paradigms emphasize compliance and discourage creativity. This paradigm fails to take advantage of the creativity and capability of the government workforce.

Leadership driven management control processes offer an alternative, additive management paradigm that seems more suited to the increasingly tight fiscal environment. This process seeks to change the status quo by creating an institutionalized, disciplined approach to maximize learning and stimulate continuous improvement in the struggle to effectively implement government missions.

The process seeks to change the organization culture so that accountability is increased in terms of two key operational questions:

1. How did you perform?
2. What are you doing to improve?

Answering these simple questions rigorously requires an understanding of resource consumption and performance that few government managers currently possess. These questions also stimulate a learning process in which the mission experts of the organization must understand the financial implications of their decisions in ways never before needed. Understanding increases the likelihood that improved methods will be found, particularly given that the leader in the leadership driven process continually asks for them.

The leadership driven management control process can coexist with current budget control processes. A more efficient situation, however, may be to use leadership driven management control exclusively at the lower operational levels. Elimination of the budget control process at lower levels of the organization should create a significant staff reduction, and it is possible that the staff savings from such an approach could fund the entire leadership driven management process. Furthermore, current attitudes about spending to budget levels and considering budgets as personal entitlements would be minimized.

The goal of the leadership is to achieve organizational missions effectively. The leadership driven management process uses learning oriented, after action reviews to continuously improve cost effectiveness in executing that mission.

CHAPTER 6

Evolving Good Cost Information

The Role and Purpose for Measurement

Leadership driven management is not based on educated guess and gut feel. The after action review process requires impartial, objective views of true levels of cost and performance.

The analogy from *Winning the Cost War*[1] is that measurement in the management control process is like reconnaissance or intelligence in the battlefield command and control process. There are several important things to learn from this analogy.

First, we know that reconnaissance alone does not win the battle. Good battlefield intelligence might very well be an essential part of a winning military strategy. However, it is only an input to the bigger command and control process. Similarly, no accounting or measurement process provides the "silver bullet" that automatically guarantees a successful management control process.

Second, many types of intelligence gathering techniques are useful to military commanders. Commanders pick and choose from radar, sonar, human intelligence, signals intelligence, scouting, infrared, unmanned aerial vehicles, and so forth, based on their needs. Similarly, leadership driven management must offer managers the choice of measurement techniques. The leader is the user, or the "customer," of the intelligence gathering, cost, and effort.

Leadership driven measurement for management control processes must be defined and bounded. The leadership driven control process described earlier is the systematic, repeated, disciplined, ongoing attention to performance. Measurements to support this process are similarly systematic, periodic, disciplined, and ongoing.

Differentiating Leadership Driven Measurement From External Reporting

Leadership driven management control processes need leadership driven management accounting. This accounting requirement differs significantly from traditional government accounting. Traditional government accounting exists solely to meet required external reporting needs.

External reporting needs are imposed by external actors powerful enough to make such information demands. Leadership driven management accounting is driven solely by leadership driven management. The development of externally reported information typically follows rigorous accounting criteria based on the external viewers' needs for consistency and comparability.

Leadership driven management accounting need only support the leadership driven management control process. This means that leadership driven management accounting's primary goals are usefulness and credibility in the management control context. Affordability adds a third requirement to leader driven management accounting, as organizations seeking cost efficiencies cannot afford to waste resources on measurement that is not useful or credible.

External reporting must pass audits designed to assure users that generally accepted accounting techniques have been rigorously followed. Leadership driven managerial accounting meets a different requirement. It must be credible to managers in representing truth. Measurement errors must be detected by the after action review process and fixed as the measurement process evolves. The difference is somewhat like that between submitting a tax return and balancing a checkbook (Figure 6.1).

Consider why you do the accounting work to complete your tax return and contrast that motivation to the accounting work required to balance your checkbook. The tax return is a personal annual financial statement that can be quite burdensome. Most people comply with this external reporting requirement because it is the law, and the law has significant penalties for noncompliance.

Balancing your checkbook, on the other hand, is entirely optional. People who elect not to do it suffer no legal penalty. Those that do balance their checkbook cite their primary motivation as needing to

External vs. Managerial

	motivation	
avoid penalties	motivation	need information
rule driven	method	customized
little or none	benefit	learning
whatever it takes	cost	minimized
risk of penalties	audit	not applicable
may be expensive	errors	fix, move on

Figure 6.1. External reporting is like filing your tax return. Managerial accounting is like balancing your checkbook. These are very different accounting processes.

know where they stand financially and that the bank has given them proper credit.

The methodology for completing your tax return is not up to you. Law rigidly defines it, and a great deal of interpretive guidance is available to help you comply with the rules. Alternatively, the exact way you balance your checkbook, if you do it, is entirely up to you. You can do it daily, weekly, monthly, or whenever you feel the need. You can do it to the penny, round to the nearest dollar, or only bother to keep within a broad range. You can also adjust your balance rather than track down every discrepancy.

Most people feel they get little benefit from the effort it takes to fill out their tax returns. People who balance their checkbook obviously feel they learn something of value or they would not bother. Furthermore, the benefit of that learning implicitly exceeds the cost of that learning or you would not expend the time and effort in the task. Completing tax returns can be costly, particularly if subcontracted, and the cost-to-benefit does not apply. This is the nature of external reporting. It is compliance driven, not value driven.

Tax audits worry people quite a bit. However, why would you cheat on your checkbook if your goal is to understand the truth of your cash flow situation? Inadvertent errors on your tax return can lead to costly penalties and great care is taken to avoid them. Inadvertent errors in your checkbook are usually discovered during the balancing process. They are quickly fixed and you move on.

The Information Needs of Leadership Driven Management Control

There is a myth that cost benefit analysis requires an accounting information system. The fact is that cost benefit analysis usually relies on estimates of future cost. It could be argued that actual cost information helps make those future cost estimates, and there is some truth there. However, designing a cost information system that would inform all potential views of cost needed for all potential decisions is unlikely to be affordable (as many implementers of activity based costing have found).

Furthermore, it seems that most cost informed decisions would likely be a one-time choice between competing alternatives. One-time decisions may be better served by ad hoc information inputs rather than by repeated, systematic measurements needed to support in leadership driven management control.

Alternatively, leadership driven management control is a continuous process and needs a continuous flow of systematic cost measurements to function. Such information supports management discovery by showing trends and enabling variance analysis. We are interested in developing useful records of reality that influence the ongoing management of the operation.

The usefulness of leadership driven managerial costing lies in the dialogue it supports regarding performance. Its value lies in providing objective insights that actors accept as representing performance. This implies that credibility and understanding are extremely important in building acceptance.

Differentiating Leadership Driven Measurement From Ad Hoc Analysis

The systematic, repeated, ongoing measurements in leadership driven managerial costing should not exclude other, additional measurements

(Figure 6.2). Ad hoc (Latin meaning "for this") measurements are also used when appropriate. Ad hoc analysis is the appropriate technique to use when management requires more detail.

These one-time analyses are a much more cost efficient way to answer special needs for information. Furthermore, an ad hoc analysis is much more likely to be further refined in its assumptions and therefore its relevancy to the particular issue under review.

On the other hand, ad hoc analyses that appear to be particularly useful may be candidates for incorporation into the systematic, periodic, disciplined, ongoing measurement process defined by management. The leadership driven measurement process evolves and adapts to management needs.

Some managerial costing designers mistakenly try to anticipate every possible ad hoc view that might be required. Doing so results in an accounting system that may cost 10 times more than needed and is likely to fail in supporting the ongoing needs of the leadership driven management control process.

The Measurement Universe

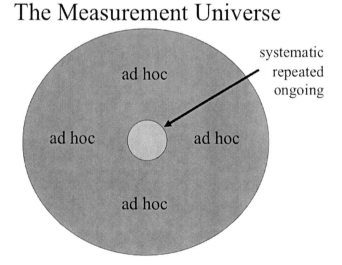

Figure 6.2. Only a small subset of all possible measurements need to be done systematically, repeatedly, and on an ongoing basis.

Relationship Between Cost of Information and Its Benefit

Information is not free. Yet the potential for information development and the resulting costs of information are infinite. These phenomena make careful consideration of the measurement strategy important.

Some organizations desiring better cost management have invested heavily in cost measurement approaches such as activity based costing. Unfortunately, many of these efforts in the government arena seem to be abandoned within a few years. Usually, the reason for abandonment is that the cost of the measurement effort exceeded its value.

Decisions in these failed efforts were likely based on the hope that cost accounting information would somehow magically transform the cost management behavior of the organization. We have tried to show here that change requires a leadership driven management approach. Measurement simply provides an input to management. It is not the silver bullet that automatically changes behavior. Only leadership driven management can change behavior. The measurement input must, at a minimum, pay for itself with beneficial use to the organization, as shown in Figure 6.3.

Minimum Cost vs. Benefit Criteria

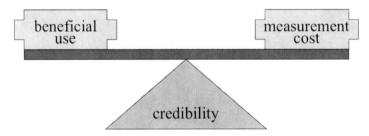

Figure 6.3. At the very least, the beneficial use of measurement should balance its cost.

However, why would an organization want to expend the time and effort in leadership driven management if it only seeks a breakeven between the cost and benefits of the program? It would seem more likely that organizations would enter into these efforts only if there were a significant residual benefit over the costs of the effort.

Figure 6.4 suggests that organizations should think in terms of a 10 to 1 ratio between benefit and cost. This kind of thinking will undoubtedly and correctly bound the complexity of planned cost accounting measurement approaches.

Measurement Specification

The practical effect of the needed 10 to 1 ratio of benefit to measurement cost is to strictly limit spending on cost measurement. This means that the number of things costed and the level of precision must be carefully considered. Affordability of the measurement process clearly limits the design of the cost measurement effort.

The affordability constraint makes design and specification of the measurement process important. Who should be responsible for measurement design also becomes an issue. Given that the benefit and value of the overall process derives from management use, it seems inescapable

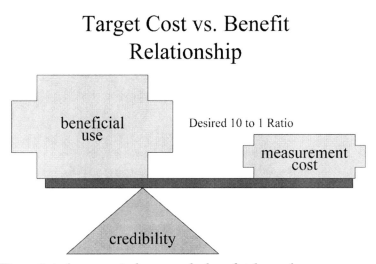

Figure 6.4. *As a practical matter, the beneficial use of cost information should greatly exceed its cost.*

that managers are the sole beneficiaries of the measurement process. Logically, managers should be the key designer of the measurement process, as they are the key user and customer of the effort.

This conclusion may be counterintuitive to accounting experts. It makes perfect sense, however, when one considers that accountable managers must "buy" information to facilitate their responsibility to improve operations. Total information is unaffordable. Perfect information is unaffordable. There is simply too much that could be measured, too many ways to measure them, and too many ways to make measurement more precise. Compromises must be made to get information sufficient to the needs of leadership driven management.

The idea of "compromising" information precision may be hard for some to accept. However, it is a very practical fact of life in many situations. We do not generally spend to measure time to microsecond levels of precision. We do not build all weight scales to gram levels of precision. Thermometers do not try to assess hundredths of a degree. When asked our age, we reply with a number of years, ignoring months, weeks, days, hours, and seconds.

We do not install speedometers on our vehicles to measure velocity in inches per second or feet per minute. We do not even try to measure acceleration. We accept the imprecision of reading analog speedometers. We do not worry about the impact of tire inflation or wear that changes tire diameter and distorts speed measurement. We accept imprecision that is "good enough for management work."

It is certainly possible technically to achieve greater levels of precision in all these cases where we tend to accept, and expect, less. We usually do not bother, for a number of reasons:

1. We do not spend to measure things that are not useful.
2. We do not spend on accuracy levels that are not useful.

Careful consideration must be given to determining the level of precision needed in building a cost measurement system. Ignoring this consideration can lead to elaborate (and expensive) cost accounting. These models may be quite elegant and are usually well done. Unfortunately, they are not leadership driven and often remain unused.

Many of the early examples of activity based costing in the Federal Government experienced this phenomenon. The models sought to cost out extremely low-level views of activities. Managers unaccustomed to any costing were simply overwhelmed by the data. Furthermore, some of these models were populated only on an annual basis. Complex allocation methodologies sometimes bewildered managers and destroyed information credibility. Annual data for very small segments of the organization did not really fit into any control process. Many of these activity based costing efforts did not survive two cycles of population. Some surviving efforts cut their granularity by a factor of 10 or more with successive model rebuilding efforts while moving from annual to quarterly or more frequent updates.

The task is further complicated by the relative inexperience with leadership driven management control in most government organizations. A much more practical strategy would be to minimize the costing measurement initiated with the implementation of leadership driven management control. This strategy reflects the fact that managers new to this type of effort do not even know what they do not know. It is impractical to think that they will be able to define the needed information specifications. Furthermore, those requirements will change as the measurement process evolves through the dynamic, interactive nature of the control process.

Recommendations

Start simply. Evolve. Do not overly complicate or delay the start-up of leadership driven management control with cost measurements that are not needed, not affordable, or not credible.

Complexity can be increased over time. However, increasing complexity should be carefully limited. Calls for complexity are sometimes made to induce delay and provide cover for people who feel threatened by the numbers. Furthermore, complexity costs and too much complexity can undermine the beneficial use of the information.

Do not try to answer all possible questions with the measurements that are required by the after action review process. Ad hoc analysis is an appropriate response to questions that can be expected to emerge from the after action review process.

Avoid the trap of substituting measurement reports and metrics for an interactive leadership driven control process. Such a mistake turns the effort into an external reporting exercise for reporters and reduces the likelihood of beneficial use. Beneficial use occurs only through the actions, decisions, and behavior changes of leadership driven managers who are learning something through their study of the measurements.

Conclusions

It is sometimes said that "dollars" represents the language of management. It is useful to think about why this might be true. The usefulness of cost measurement is that all sorts of things can be translated into dollars. People, contracts, purchases can all be measured in dollars. Once so measured, it is possible to add people and purchases, apples and oranges together. It is then possible to make tradeoffs or substitutions between one category of expenditure and another.

Measurement's importance to leadership driven cost management and control lies in its ability to facilitate the process with credible rendering of the facts so that managers can and will take actions that lead to improvement.

CHAPTER 7

Organization Based Operational Control Processes

Introduction

All organizations have organization (org) charts, and they are powerful things. This graphical depiction of reporting relationships says a lot about the organization and, more importantly, how it works. Its mere existence reflects the need for a hierarchy of accountability: the chain of command. It also shows the perceived best practice of segregating tasks and organizing work to accomplish the organization's missions. As such, the org chart provides a natural basis for financial management and control.

A cost managed organization using an organization based control process takes advantage of the reporting relationships embedded in the org chart. Subordinates report their organization's achievements, results, and improvements. It is important that the management-subordinate team periodically meet to interact regarding the issues in the after action review process.

The basic reporting requirement can be described simply as "show and tell." This means showing what the organization is doing to improve the efficiency and effectiveness of its operations and telling the story of the previous period's financial performance.

Organization based control processes that use the chain of command implicitly change management processes in the direction of greater decentralization. Rule based management has less use for decentralization. Rules promulgated at the top cascade through the entire organization, lessening the role of middle management.

Decentralized Management Control

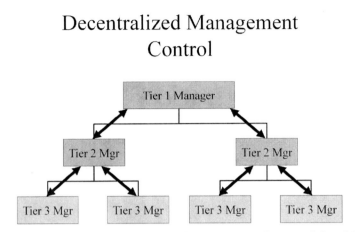

Figure 7.1. Results from Tier 3 performance must be consolidated for the Tier 2 manager's after action review with the Tier 1 manager.

Consider the simple org chart in Figure 7.1. Traditional centralized operating practice at many federal organizations sees Tier 3 managers looking for policy and rule making from the Tier 1 manager. The Tier 3 manager then simply "complies" with the policies of central management.

The double-headed arrows represent the organization based control process where the subordinate manager presents results to higher level management. This represents a major change from past practice and works to strengthen the chain of command. It also places new demands on managers of managers. Tier 2 managers in Figure 7.1 now have more authority in directing their Tier 3 subordinates, and that authority comes with a much greater responsibility for their results.

The power of the process lies in the learning and leadership driven improvement that occurs throughout the organization. Many, if not most, of the ideas and initiatives for improvement will come from the lower levels of the organization, those most stifled by the centralization of policy and the process of compliance with rules. (See Figure 7.2.)

Unique Scope Considerations

Organization based control processes are typically broad in scope compared with the role based control processes described in chapter 9. Role based processes are focused at a role defined interface (such as the interface

The Power of Decentralization

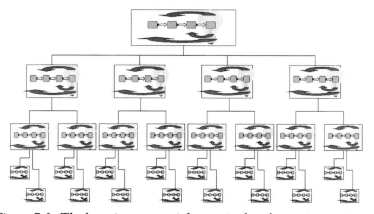

Figure 7.2. The learning process inherent in the after action review achieves great power as it cascades down the organization chart.

between support and line functions) and involve relatively few, but senior, managers. Likewise, output based control described in chapter 11, while more complicated from a measurement perspective, is often limited to a relative handful of higher level managers with comprehensive output focused responsibility. Organization based processes, however, can, and typically do, involve all personnel with supervisory responsibilities.

The relatively massive scope and broad inclusiveness mean that successful implementation of organization based control processes requires a significant culture change. On the other hand, the broad scope promises significant and persistent return on investment. Moreover, organization based control also provides an important communication mechanism and management tool capable of energizing the complete chain of command in ways that probably do not currently exist.

The comprehensiveness of the org chart means that organization based control processes are potentially the largest and most important management control processes for government organizations. Each node on the org chart above the lowest level presents an opportunity for an after action review.

Consider, for example, an organization with three tiers where every manager supervises five subordinate organizations. As shown in Table 7.1, there would be 25 Tier 3 suborganizations. The after action review cycle would see five meetings with Tier 3 managers presenting to Tier 2 managers and one after action review where the Tier 2 managers are presenting to the Tier 1 manager.

Of course, the total number of after action reviews grows rapidly as the number of tiers expands. An organization with six tiers would expect 781 after action reviews each reporting cycle, a substantial task to organize and execute.

Unique Behavioral Dimensions

The process differs significantly from many accountability processes in government in that the desired results are not and cannot be specifically defined. The twin goals of understanding costs and generating continuous improvement can be stated only in broad terms. Specifics are hard, if not impossible, to define.

Even the highest level, brightest, or most experienced leaders cannot direct specific continuous improvement initiatives. However, there is much that leaders can do to stimulate the self-motivated creativity that leads to continuous improvement.

Most importantly, leaders can ask for improvements. As simple as this sounds, many government employees report that they have never been

Table 7.1.

	3-Tier Org	4-Tier Org	5-Tier Org	6-Tier Org
Tier 1 Entities	1	1	1	1
Tier 2 Entities	5	5	5	5
Tier 3 Entities	25	25	25	25
Tier 4 Entities		125	125	125
Tier 5 Entities			625	625
Tier 6 Entities				3,125
Total Number After Action Reviews	6	31	156	781
The number of after action reviews increases rapidly as the number of organization levels increases.				

asked for process improvement suggestions. Certainly, if no one asks for improvement ideas, it is unlikely that many will be forthcoming.

It also seems clear that expecting new ideas increases the likelihood of getting them. Leaders should understand that their subordinates are the experts in what they do and expect that they should be able to find better ways of doing things. Furthermore, it is not unreasonable to expect that there are always better ways of doing things: the underlying philosophy of continuous improvement.

Asking for creative thinking is good. Expecting continuous improvement is better. Institutionalizing the generation of new ideas is one of the goals of the after action review process. This process provides the forum for leaders to review new idea generation and signal the importance of continuous improvement. It also provides leaders with the opportunity to evaluate the continuous improvement capabilities of their subordinates.

Some subordinates are likely to find this open-ended requirement difficult. They, like many students, prefer to know the performance expectation in great detail so that their responsibility is merely to comply with the requirement.

The expectation here demands significantly more. It requires that each subordinate embrace the goal of continuous improvement and self-direct their actions as well as motivating self-directed efforts of their subordinates toward this never-ending quest. The goal is to enable and expect greater creative initiative throughout the organization. After all, critical expertise exists deep within the organization, not with senior executives and political appointees. (See Figure 7.3.)

Essential Requirement: Leadership Driven Management

While all management control processes must be leadership driven, the organization based control process requires much more leadership than others. Leadership is vital here because of the number of managers involved as the process cascades down the org chart. Success requires that the critical responsibilities of all managers change. Leaders at all levels must evaluate their subordinates on two key requirements:

1. Does the subordinate understand the financial aspects of resource consumption?

Comparing Control Philosophies

Centralized Control	Org Based Control
• Management – Specifies Task Details	• Management – Specifies Continuous Improvement Goals
• Subordinate – Complies With Specification	• Subordinate – Self-Directs Tasks
• Control – Note Compliance	• Control – Evaluate Results and Capabilities

Figure 7.3. Rule driven management encourages only compliance, while leadership driven management expects more thinking and creativity from employees.

2. Does the subordinate demonstrate a capable creativity in identifying, implementing, and achieving continuous improvement?

The new responsibility set requires that subordinates understand how their fiscal resources are consumed. Earlier, we identified four requirements for successful leadership driven control: (a) leaders, (b) staff, (c) process, and (d) measurement. It should be clear that the goal of staff, process, and measurement is to facilitate managerial learning regarding how resources are spent. Leaders must evaluate and assess how their subordinates perform in this regard.

Capable creativity is the other key demand. Subordinates must demonstrate that they and their organizations can make improvement happen. This is an open-ended and undefined requirement in terms of the details of what this capable creativity will achieve. It is simply impossible to specify exactly what should be done. Organizations are too diverse, environments are different, and opportunities for new thinking too numerous. It is impossible to define the substance of new creativity. However, creativity itself can be required and evaluated.

These requirements are broad and somewhat ambiguous compared with many government requirements. This means that judgment will be required. It is likely that this judgment capability will be relatively undeveloped in most organizations at the start of an organization based control process. Developing this capability is an important element of success. It should be recognized, however, that failure to motivate one's subordinates will likely result in failure to impress one's superior.

It should also be clear that the cost chain of command is only as strong as its weakest link (Figure 7.4). An incompetent or process-resistant middle manager effectively breaks the chain and blocks his subordinate organizations from achieving their potential. The impact worsens when the break occurs higher in the chain of command. Perhaps the most important leadership responsibility of senior management is to critically evaluate the competency of their immediate subordinates.

Unique Measurement Considerations

Many, if not most, organizations track financial transactions by organization element. Accounting databases therefore reflect, or can fairly easily be rearranged to reflect, cost by organization element. Each block on the

Cost Chain of Command

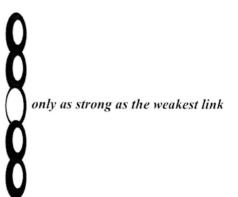

Tier One

Tier Two

Tier Three   *only as strong as the weakest link*

Tier Four

Tier Five

Figure 7.4. The cost chain of command is only as strong as its weakest link.

org chart represents a cost center or a consolidation of subordinate cost centers. The org chart itself can be thought of as depicting the reporting relationships that include all the organization's cost centers and cost center managers.

Consolidation Issues

The hierarchical nature of organization based control requires some special consideration of measurement consolidation. Reporting of results inherently follows a bottom-to-top sequence. In other words, it makes more sense for the Tier 2 manager in the Figure 7.1 org chart to first review his subordinate organizations before presenting to higher management. Clearly, some consolidation of results from subordinate organizations is also a prerequisite.

A number of consolidation issues demand consideration. These are the use of eliminations entities to avoid double counting, the use of judgment entities to mitigate the challenge of aggressive plans, and the use of other entities to hold certain costs at higher organization levels.

"Eliminations" Entities

It is often the case that one part of an organization uses the services of another. Sometimes these relationships are formalized with internal service agreements (ISAs). The possibility exists that cost is double counted if one subordinate organization records cost for the ISA and another records the cost of labor and materials to provide the service.

The accounting solution to prevent double counting is "elimination" accounting. Visualize a third, virtual suborganization called the eliminations entity. Its purpose is to record an offset to the cost of the ISA. Consolidation of the three entities now restates things correctly for the sum of the suborganization pieces.

"Judgment" Entities

High-performing organizations often achieve their results by giving subordinate organizations challenging financial goals. However, the risk of missing goals increases with challenge. A "judgment" entity offsets some of the challenge of planned performance so that the consolidation of challenged suborganizations and the judgment entity is less aggressive.

A judgment entity might also be used to accumulate accounting reserves for contingent liabilities that management desires to hold at the consolidated level rather than distribute to lower levels. This mechanism could also apply to year-end transactions where time considerations make it more practical to leave obligations at the higher level.

"Other" Entities

An "other" entity might also be used to book charges that the consolidated entity does not wish to distribute. For example, the role based control process may allocate these costs to major organization segments. That high-level entity may or may not decide to push those costs down to subordinate organizations. This is particularly likely when the support cost is completely noncontrollable by the subordinate entity: agency overhead, for example.

Unique Accountability Considerations

Many, if not most, organizations conduct employee performance reviews through the organization hierarchy. Managers and supervisors are accustomed to evaluating their subordinates and being evaluated by higher levels on the org chart. Human resource departments already run an infrastructure of performance appraisal, usually combined with compensation management. Again, this provides a natural setting for leadership driven financial management by simply adding financial performance to the evaluation criteria and the performance appraisal process.

The inclusiveness of organization based control processes make them ideal options for organization-wide efforts to improve operational performance. Institutionalizing control processes in this format proves particularly effective in driving continuous improvement programs.

Tracking Savings and Benefits

Organization based control processes must provide savings and benefits far in excess of the costs of implementing and maintaining the process.

While tracking those savings and benefits is important, it does not make a lot of sense to spend much of the savings on the tracking process. Furthermore, it will often be the case that benefits can be difficult to determine. Therefore, it is reasonable to think about the different types of savings and benefits and how they will be tracked.

Some savings are clearly defined and obvious. Eliminating an employee position, for example, is a "hard dollar" saving. The benefit of changing an employee's responsibilities to improve the organization's process is harder to evaluate. Both are desirable outcomes and should be encouraged. However, tracking mechanisms and the goal setting processes should differ.

Hard dollar savings enable definitive targets and can be tracked relatively easily. This type of savings can be verified by control staff without much effort or cost. Furthermore, hard dollar savings can be reprogrammed or redirected on a dollar-for-dollar basis. In fact, documenting and publicizing the reprogramming can be a powerful motivator as well as very positive recognition.

The soft dollar savings due to process improvements represent more of a cost avoidance than real savings. Trying to measure the value of these savings usually requires making some assumptions. The dollar difference between conservative and liberal assumptions can be significant. While outrageous assumptions and inflated savings claims are not good, there is probably more to lose by being too conservative.

The most important thing is to have this problem in the first place. It is more than likely that a somewhat liberal calculation of savings will do much to encourage, motivate, and recognize good work. There is little downside from overestimating, as long as it is understood that these are not "hard dollar" savings that can be redirected.

Conclusions

Implementing an organization based control process requires a massive culture change. Furthermore, it is likely that this process could require 5 to 10 years to achieve maturity. The transformation will probably not occur by simply issuing a policy or by writing a rule.

Success requires the absolute commitment and dedication of leadership. Perhaps the most important recommendation is not to attempt an organization based control process without the interest, advocacy, and active engagement of leaders.

Even with good leadership, the transition will not be easy. The following case study shows how the United States Army Garrison at Fort Huachuca, Arizona, accomplished its successful transition.

CHAPTER 8

Fort Huachuca U.S. Army Garrison

Case Study

Introduction

Fort Huachuca is an Army installation located southeast of Tucson, Arizona. Its location made it ideal to monitor Apache comings and goings through the San Pedro Mountains and as a staging point for General Pershing's punitive mission into Mexico. In this role, it was home to some of the famous Buffalo Soldiers who played a significant role in "winning the West."

Today, the installation houses the U.S. Army's Military Intelligence School and the troops of a Signal Corps Brigade. The "garrison" organization runs the support and sustainment functions of the installation. It is typically led by a colonel, although most of the garrison staff is civilian. The Fort Huachuca Garrison hosted a pilot effort by the U.S. Army to implement improved cost management and control processes capable of "winning the cost war."

This case study will present the evolution of an organization based cost management and control process within the Fort Huachuca Garrison. It will approach the task chronologically and highlight the motivations, concerns, and contributions of a succession of Garrison Commanders.

Start-Up and Early Years, 1996–2000

As budgets get cut year after year, it seems to me that there has to be a better way to use increasingly limited resources. There must be a systematic management process of continuous improvement that would be far better than mindlessly cutting x% of our capability every time there's an x% budget cut.

—Jim Freauff, Internal Review Director, Fort Huachuca

Interest in cost management began with Jim Freauff, the Director of Internal Review. The Internal Review Department is an audit-like function that reports to the Garrison Commander. It is responsible for special studies related to the operation of the entire installation, but as a practical matter spends most of its efforts as the analytic arm of the Garrison Commander in review of garrison functions.[1]

Although an accountant who had spent his career in government accounting and audit roles, Freauff's first exposure to activity based cost accounting came at a conference of Army Internal Review people at St. Louis in the spring of 1996. One of the speakers was from Fort Bragg, North Carolina, which had started some activity based costing. It looked like the solution to a cost tracking project that Freauff was currently addressing with spreadsheets.

After the conference he visited Fort Bragg and met with the contractor implementing the activity based cost system. He requested a bid from the contractor and immediately rejected it as far out of line with his limited resources. Freauff then contacted the software vendor, ABC Technologies, and contracted to buy a few days of "rapid prototyping" assistance and some software to do a pilot effort.

The area selected for the rapid prototyping effort was the Directorate of Logistics. This roughly $9 million per year function provided vehicle maintenance, ammunition handling, dining hall, laundry, and many other support services essential to the operation of a large military installation. The team spent three days learning activity based costing and the ABC Technologies software product. They also built an activity based costing model of the Directorate and briefed it to the Garrison Commander, Colonel Elliot, on the last day.

Freauff's reaction of the initial effort was "this isn't that difficult." However, Colonel Elliot had finished his tour of duty at Fort Huachuca and Colonel Chopin replaced him in July 1996. Change in command often results in canceling the previous commander's initiatives and beginning a new set. Those who are opposed to change know that oftentimes they must simply "wait out" the current command to prevail. Freauff briefed his new boss on the effort and was pleased that the initiative was not going to end with his previous boss's end of command. Colonel Chopin supported the effort and approved development of a full model for the Logistics Directorate.

The First Model

Freauff and his staff spent most of the next six months expanding and refining the activity based cost model for the Directorate of Logistics. This Directorate was a fairly complex organization.

Activity based costing seeks an accounting of cost by the activities performed. While traditional costing might view cost by payroll, travel, contracts, supplies, and so forth, activity based costing views cost by function. Managers had been used to seeing the budget in the more traditional view. Building the ABC model required a logical reorganization of the costs.

The ABC Tech software starts with the traditional view of costs. This view, known as the resource module, is then cross-charged into a different structure of activities. Activities can then be further transformed into a view of cost by cost objects. For example, a resource module at Ford Motor Company would contain direct labor payroll that might then flow to labor activities, such as welding, painting, and setting up machines. Each of these activities might then flow to cost objects representing each car model produced.

Deciding what is an activity and what is not an activity is more difficult than it seems. One might, for example, consider answering the phone, making copies, and other similar tasks as activities. A cost system can certainly be built on this basis, but Freauff and the Logistics staff assigned to model building quickly rejected this approach as meaningless. They instead chose to develop a view of activities that would capture the functions and services provided.

Deciding on the scope of an activity is also a nontrivial decision. Some managers wanted the model to capture the complexity of their organizations and, indirectly, the difficulty of their jobs. For example, preparing vegetables was considered an important activity in the food preparation process. The supervisor of this area thought that perhaps there should be separate activities for each vegetable: preparing potatoes, preparing carrots, preparing beans, and so forth. The preparing potato activity then could be subdivided into types of preparation: preparing mashed potatoes, preparing baked potatoes, preparing French fried potatoes, and so forth. Each of these activities could further be divided into finer views of costs by process: washing potatoes for mashed potatoes, peeling potatoes for mashed potatoes, cutting potatoes for mashed potatoes, and so forth. The entire activity (which totaled $14,000 per year) could have been split into scores of minor activities with little added benefit and much added effort and cost.

The team had to decide how to bound activities in meaningful ways. Freauff later remarked that "fortunately the budget to do this task was small and the time allotted was short. We didn't go down the path of creating a cost accounting monument to vegetable preparation." Yet the Directorate was fairly large, and when completed, the model contained 350 activities. Table 8.1 shows a more consolidated view of annual costs in thousands of dollars.

Building the model did not stop with the definition of the activity structure. Mechanisms had to be established to allocate, assign, or trace the use of resources by activities in order to calculate the activity cost view. After several months of work, the model was ready to accept data, and Freauff began to manually load accounting data from the end-of-year reports of the Defense Department's Standard Financial System (STANFINS).

Table 8.1.

Perform Maintenance	$2,772
Provide Transportation	$2,016
Provide Retail Supplies	$1,308
Provide Food Services	$1,068
Provide Laundry Services	$600
Manage Assets	$504
Provide Combat Supplies	$252
Provide Ammunition	$168
Total	$8,688

Freauff was justifiably proud of the ABC model, his first. He built it at a fraction of the cost asked for by the consultant and in a fraction of the time that a consulting team would have taken. He felt the model had the right balance of complexity and relevancy. It presented never-before-seen views of cost that he thought to be of great value.

The First Attempt at Management Interaction

In December 1996, Freauff staged a briefing for Colonel Chopin by the managers from the Directorate of Logistics. Using annual cost data from fiscal year 1995 that ended in September, managers attempted to explain their costs, without much success, enthusiasm, or enlightenment.

Freauff was very disappointed.

> The meeting was an absolute disaster. We built a great model, but managers claimed they didn't understand it. Certainly, there was no sense of ownership. The managers simply didn't accept that the numbers were their numbers. They were critical of the whole process and particularly of the fact that the numbers were for an entire year.

Most managers thought the entire effort a waste of time. They considered the activity based costing effort to be simply an initiative of a new commander attempting to distinguish himself and his career.

Being measured in itself caused negative reactions because measurement was obviously a prerequisite to accountability. One participant privately related that he believed management "finally found a way to measure us individually in order to get rid of us." He approached the effort with the feeling that the purpose of the cost data was "to be used against us."

Another manager felt ABC was just "another acronymed program." Still another remembered her first reaction in hearing about ABC.

> This appeared to be just another tasker. Everybody grumbled about the work and said "we already do that." It is not going to work for us. Most people left the training unsold on the value of

the effort. We had the typical civil servant attitude—we will just wait out the commander and his initiative.

It appears that roughly 40% of the participants openly rejected the value of the process. Another 40% approached it passively. Even those who saw value in the measurement effort questioned whether the time and work required justified the results.

Emergence of Leadership Driven Management

When I took command it was clear that I had no real way of impacting much. All the budget was distributed to my subordinates and there was nothing left to play with. I needed a process that would free up resources for me to command if I was going to make a contribution personally.

—Colonel Ted Chopin, Garrison Commander, Fort Huachuca

Colonel Chopin reported for duty as the Garrison Commander in July 1996. His area of expertise was military intelligence, and he had served extensively in Europe. His experience in military intelligence led to selection as a Director's Fellow at the National Security Agency, where he served 3 years. He was a rated pilot for both fixed and rotary wing aircraft.

Chopin's impression of the first attempt at management interaction was not as bad as Freauff's. He simply expected less. As a military intelligence specialist, he believed that cost measurements were analogous to pieces of gathered intelligence. He knew that information, by itself, was incapable of action or results. He recognized that people would be the key to using the gathered intelligence effectively, and he accepted the role of motivating and teaching the staff.

Chopin saw cost management as a way to impact his command. Whereas the traditional process focused on spending the budget, cost management focused on costs and finding more efficient ways to accomplish the mission. He saw the potential to free up resources for needs that were not in the budget and create a command difference.

One of the participants at the first review remembered his first impressions of the Garrison Commander.

Colonel Chopin was a real used car salesman. He believed in cost management and when he told us that he had been trained in the subject as part of his pre-command training we started to understand that ABC wasn't just another passing fad.

Colonel Chopin did not scrap the program as many expected. Instead, he secured $249K funding from the Training and Doctrine Command, the headquarters entity of Fort Huachuca and the Military Intelligence School. He authorized a remodeling effort for the Logistics Directorate and model-building efforts for the other directorates under his command.

In August 1997, the Cost and Economic Analysis Center, an Army staff group, sought a location to experiment with ideas in using cost measurement in a cost based management process. They asked both Forts Bragg and Huachuca if they wished to be the pilot site. The speed and enthusiasm in Fort Huachuca's response secured the pilot.

Cost Management Training

Cost management recognizes that cost measurement does not automatically mean that cost management occurs.[2] It emphasizes that cost measurement is simply a reconnaissance process: something that Colonel Chopin quickly understood. The cost management training presented a simple closed loop feedback process.

The process begins with a plan for spending in the immediate future. The length of the period being planned is optional. Planning by quarter and by month was discussed. It was decided to plan initially by month to increase the learning from the process and revisit the issue after the process was established.

The training took place in September 1997 for the Directorate of Logistics: the area with the most developed cost measurement process and the designated pilot area for the cost based management pilot. The Directorate was tasked to complete their cost plan for November spending by the end of October.

The most important part of the cost management process is the after action review. This review occurs after the previously planned time period has ended and actual cost results are available. The goal of the review is to institutionalize a learning process that results in better cost measurement, better cost planning, and better cost spending.

The First After Action Review

Chopin and Freauff carefully considered the format to issue for the after action review. They decided that it should be simple. They also required the plan to show overhead cost within the directorate in a way that would emphasize cost of overhead in proportion to the direct costs. Figure 7.4 shows an actual slide from the first presentation that illustrates the numeric simplicity of the required presentation format.

The first after action review at Fort Huachuca took place in early November 1997. The review compared the actual costs for the month of October with the plan approved approximately a month earlier. Overall results showed that the directorate had spent $62K less than planned. Freauff noted that this was almost 10% less than anticipated and that if annualized the underspending would total roughly three quarters of a million dollars! Figure 8.1 shows summary data from that first meeting.

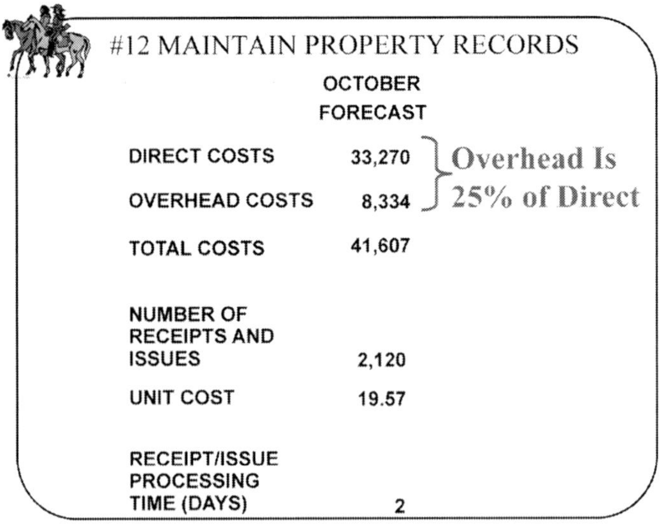

Figure 8.1. Colonel Chopin specified this format because he wanted his subordinates to think more about internal overhead.

Significant Variances

Activity (Work Center)	Plan	Actual	Variance	Percentage
T-Bird Dining Facilities	33.9	21.1	12.8	38%
Warehouse	32.9	22.8	10.1	31%
Contract Dining Facilities	57.2	44.0	13.2	23%
General Purpose Maint	13.5	10.5	3.0	22%
ADP Government	11.1	9.1	2.0	18%
Special Purpose Maint	39.1	33.2	5.9	15%
Personal Property	64.9	58.1	6.8	10%
Laundry	38.2	34.6	3.6	9%
Tactical Maint	70.3	65.8	4.5	6%
All others	355.9	355.8	0.1	0%
Total Variance			62.0	

Figure 8.2. The first review showed some interesting and unexpected results. The T-Bird Dining Hall significantly underspent its plan.

Most managers did not spend a great deal of time on their plan. They simply assumed that the spending for October would be one twelfth the annual budget. The view of overhead did get the anticipated attention. Supervisors were stunned in some cases to see that overhead coming only from their own directorate was 30% or 40% of their direct costs. It was obvious that they were starting to think about costs in a different way.

Individual managers took the floor to explain "their" numbers. Most were uncomfortable with this requirement: they had never been asked to explain their operations in financial terms. The usual process was for their budget officer to advise them periodically throughout the year if they were spending at too high or too low a rate. They would also go to the budget officer if they wished to buy something to see whether it was affordable. Their level of understanding of the financial consequences of their decisions was minimal.

It was also clear that cost improvement opportunities existed. Note from Figure 8.2 that the supervisor of the T-Bird Dining Hall was roughly 40% favorable to his plan. When asked how he could plan so much higher just a month earlier, he admitted that he had simply divided his annual budget by 12. Colonel Chopin replied that such a planning process was acceptable for this cycle but pressed on why such large a favorable result had occurred. Gradually, the story emerged. It developed that the signal corps brigade had gone to Egypt on special training maneuvers for most of the month and he had not known in advance.

Colonel Chopin immediately responded that training events of such magnitude were established months in advance, that they were not secret, and that such events provided obvious opportunities to reduce staff, cut costs, do preventative maintenance, and so forth. The message was clear: "You can't manage cost unless you think ahead and anticipate."

Another presenter, a supervisor from a contractor company that did much of the logistics work, used the forum to test the response to cost improvement suggestions. He said,

> You know, Colonel Chopin, we are required by contract to account for miscellaneous property like staplers. This requirement can't be adding much value to the Garrison. Furthermore, we had an employee doing this job who just left her job. If we don't replace her and drop this requirement we can save you $23K per year.

Colonel Chopin's response was immediate:

> Great job. You know the computers you've wanted for the warehouse that we haven't been able to afford. Well, you just funded them with this idea. Take $6K and get them immediately. They are now funded and I will make good use of the rest of the savings at the Garrison level. You are a great American.

Then the contract manager, the supervisor of the presenter, spoke up. He suggested that the idea be included in the next rebid of the contract due in 6 months. Colonel Chopin used the opportunity to teach another lesson. He responded,

> Well you are here and my contracts manager is here. Why don't you two get together tomorrow and figure out how to modify the existing contract to get this savings right away. We shouldn't waste the opportunity to save money we need to reapply to other needs.

Accounting Information Issues

While some great things happened at the review, many of the managers had difficulty explaining or even understanding "their" numbers. Much of this was due to the nature of the obligation tracking system. By law, funds must be considered encumbered (not available for other use) when a legal obligation to spend exists. That means that the entire amount of an annual contract could be entered into the obligation accounting system at the beginning of the year when the contract is signed.

This made it very difficult for the ABC models to determine activity costs for a one-month or one-quarter period of time. Some of the accounting data, such as civilian payroll, was closely correlated to the "actual" consumption of resources. Other entries, such as contracts, were not.

An additional problem was that sometimes costs were incurred that benefited more than one cost center. For example, the Directorate of Installation Support might provide building repairs for the Directorate of Logistics. There was an accounting process to transfer the costs incurred by Installation Support to Logistics, but the process was lengthy and was often not completed until the year-end closing. STANFINS was designed to deliver information that was accurate on an annual basis.

Furthermore, STANFINS did not even track military payroll. That was maintained on a completely different system, with a completely different budget. Manual adjustments were made to include these costs based on the average cost by rank of military personnel working in the garrison.

Some managers saw this as an opportunity to resist the cost management process. One stated, "We're comparing apples (the monthly plan) to oranges (the accounting data.)" Colonel Chopin's response to this was, "As long as 95% of the apples correspond to 95% of the oranges, that's okay. If not, then we need to address the issue." This signaled that accounting anomalies would not be considered an acceptable explanation at the next cost review.

Managers and budget officers also had legitimate complaints about the ABC workload. Many believed that their functions had been cut to the bone already. Not only were they resistant to the idea that they needed to become more efficient, but they struggled with the added tasks of building ABC models and updating the driver data frequently.

The accounting information issues stimulated a redo of the costing model. Less complexity in the model was thought to simplify the accounting problem. The new model for the Logistics Directorate, for example, dropped to 125 activities from its original 350.

The Next Year

One year later Colonel Chopin was preparing for his next assignment. He was now into his third year as Garrison Commander, having already extended the tour from its normal 2-year tenure. He considered it one of the best, and most rewarding, jobs he had done.

By this time, the "Quarterly Training Brief," or QTB, was an established process. Colonel Chopin pointed out that the cycle of planning, performance, and review was part of Army doctrine, but now they were applying it to cost performance instead of battlefield performance. (See Figure 8.3.)

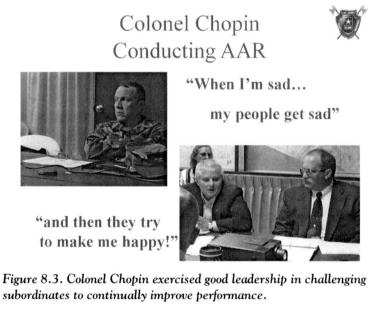

Figure 8.3. Colonel Chopin exercised good leadership in challenging subordinates to continually improve performance.

As well as the first meeting had gone, the second was even better. Eighteen cost improvement initiatives had been presented, and 17 of them were implemented. After 6 months, he was confident that his command could easily absorb the worst-case budget cut expected in the next fiscal year, and he was already reprogramming savings into important, but unfunded, quality-of-life and information technology projects. He estimated that cost reductions would total 15% by the end of the first year of implementation.

Based on these results, Colonel Chopin was invited to speak at a Defense Department conference. He emphasized that cost management required a culture change in three ways. First, managers must "divorce" themselves from the traditional budget emphasis. Second, managers must substitute a focus on cost and performance. Third, managers must be held accountable for results.

The results achieved also came to the attention of the Army's top commander, Chief of Staff General Reimer. General Reimer decided to visit Fort Huachuca to better understand the process. He said, "It briefs well, but I want to hear from the people on how it really works." As he left, apparently satisfied, his aide commented, "It is exciting: what you have done is unleash the creativity of your people."

The First Transition

Even though the activity based model and the cost management process were now implemented throughout the garrison, they were far from institutionalized. Many managers were still very uncomfortable with the process, and some were publicly critical of it. The workload involved was still significant and to some it seemed like they were setting themselves up for criticism. Some still thought the process was a personal attack. This feeling was probably increased when one of the senior managers found alternative employment after a "counseling" session from Colonel Chopin that was at least partially due to his poor response to the cost management program.

Civilian employees had seen many officers come and go. Many looked forward to Colonel Chopin's leaving. Would the new commander scrap the initiatives of his predecessor and seek to define his own tenure with a new program?

Freauff worried that the change in command would be the end of the program. To maximize the chance of a successful transition, he and Colonel Chopin made special efforts to brief Colonel Mike Boardman, the incoming Garrison Commander, on his precommand visit. The objective of the briefing was to convince Colonel Boardman that something good had been achieved and that it should be continued.

Institutionalizing Cost Management and Control

Oh my God. What have I gotten myself into? I was used to dealing with millions of dollars in my prior assignment and now I am going to be dealing with the dollar and cents cost per plumbing work order. Nothing in my career prepared me for this job."

—Colonel Mike Boardman, Garrison Commander, Fort Huachuca

Colonel Boardman remembers this reaction after visiting Fort Huachuca before his change-of-command ceremony and sitting in on an after action review. Boardman had 21 years of Army service upon taking command. He was an ROTC graduate who completed law school and practiced a couple years before fulfilling his 4-year obligation as a military intelligence officer.

When his obligation was completed, he decided that he liked the Army and chose to go to the Army Special Forces school instead of returning to the legal profession. After a tour of duty in Special Forces, he served as a paratrooper in the 82nd Airborne Division. He saw combat in Operation Desert Storm in G2 Operations of the 3rd Armored Division and was awarded the Bronze Star. Before coming to Fort Huachuca as Garrison Commander, he served as the top military intelligence officer for U.S. Army Europe.

Although the details of his first after action review seemed somewhat daunting, he was not "overwhelmed by the money." He had dealt with much larger sums in previous assignments and considered himself good at acquiring and spending money. Now he "got interested in cost management and saw it was good."

Although he was impressed by the cost measurement process, he was surprised that performance measurements were lacking. His tactical motto during his career had been "what are we supposed to do and how do we know when we've done it." Applying this maxim to cost management, he saw the need for both cost measurement and performance measurement.

The cost management process under Colonel Boardman evolved to meet his needs. Increased emphasis was placed on measuring the outputs and accomplishments of activities. While the measuring outputs increased the measurement burden, significant steps were taken to reduce the measurement workload by developing automated tools and easy-to-read graphical representations of numbers.

He felt that Colonel Chopin, his predecessor, had focused more on deploying the system and Colonel Boardman wanted to add his own input. He decided not to lead by reviewing detailed reports from supervisors. He chose to hold directors more accountable and stay out of the details. He said,

> I saw right away that directors would bring their talking mouth pieces to the meetings and avoid any real accountability. Maybe it was basic human laziness, but I didn't want to spend so much time in so many meetings where the directors were sitting like a stump on a log. I am focusing on motivating people.

His approach seemed to work. The garrison generated more than 100 cost avoidance and cost reduction initiatives in his first year. Most of these he saw as "blinding flashes of the obvious." There are "still lots of low hanging fruit." When directors claimed that quality suffered by cost reduction, he modified his approach to also stress performance improvement and not just cost reduction.

Colonel Boardman described the cost management process as

> a sailboat tacking into the wind. As long as the hand is firmly on the rudder and the sail set in the right direction it is possible to make good headway. However, you know what happens as soon as you take your hand off the tiller. Things immediately go backwards.

Colonel Boardman firmly believed that cost management was important: "We need to change the current environment where it is not important how money is spent." Yet he worried that the process was still not institutionalized and wondered what the next change of command would bring. "My successor might be a guy who says 'what's this crap'—I'm an Army officer." He felt that another problem hurting the long-term success of program implementation was the lack of interest from his superiors. He relayed that there is "only passive support" and very little appreciation for the cost management accomplishments that have been achieved. Nevertheless, he organized a transition program like the one he had received so that his successor would see the value of continuing the effort.

Evolution of Cost Control

Colonel Larry Portouw took command of the garrison at Fort Huachuca in the fall of 2002. At his first staff meeting, he emphasized the need to continue and further develop the cost management program. He also decided to make his mark on the cost management and control process by building systems tools to facilitate the tracking and communication of information used at the after action review. By this time, the review was called the Garrison Management Review and Colonel Portouw commissioned building of the Garrison Management System. (See Figure 8.4.)

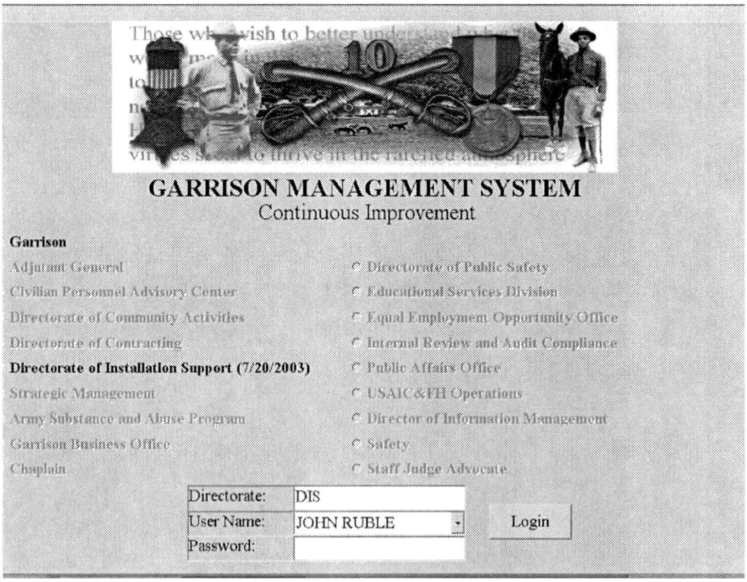

Figure 8.4. The Garrison Management System pulled cost and performance measurements together in a manner prescribed by managers who used the system.

The Garrison Management System did much to institutionalize the cost management and control process. As shown in Figure 8.5, it made it easy to see cost trends of the efforts and activities in organizations. Each organization tracked costs and output of their major activities. Slides like this were used in the quarterly garrison cost reviews.

The system tracked and displayed eight quarters of costs and outputs. Directorate managers would display areas that they thought were important. Colonel Portouw would also come to the meeting prebriefed by Freauff and with questions of his own. Colonel Portouw's meeting agenda was also refined so that each presenter had 20 minutes, and the entire meeting took one morning each quarter.

The first item on the agenda required each directorate manager to discuss his progress toward an annual goal of 2% measurable cost savings. Next, each displayed his cost improvement initiatives and processes that were being reviewed. Managers also discussed the progress toward implementation. By this time the garrison was generating 60 to 80 new improvement projects per quarter that provided between $3 million and $4 million in savings and avoidances.

The agenda then asked directorate managers to show how they were reprogramming cost savings to their unfunded requirements. Colonel

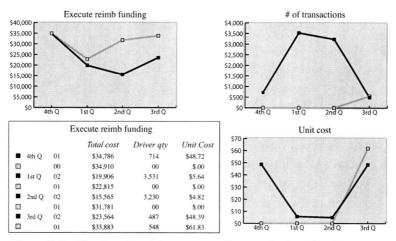

Figure 8.5. The Garrison Management System displayed eight quarters of cost, output, and unit cost information and presented the information in an easy-to-understand fashion.

Portouw's philosophy was that all savings could stay with the improving organization. He felt this improved their motivation. Displaying the redirecting of savings also increased the perceived value of the cost management and control process.

The presentation then shifted to the productivity review enabled by the Garrison Management System. This part of the review inevitably took the most time. The presentation closed with a look at directorate overhead, an issue area begun during Colonel Chopin's tenure but still deemed important.

Colonel Portouw left the program much more systematized and established. He also continued the transition plan to ensure his successor continued to build on the foundation.

Biggest Challenge

Colonel Jonathon Hunter assumed garrison command in the fall of 2004. He had previous experience as commander of a smaller garrison in Korea and sought the assignment to Fort Huachuca.

By now, the cost control and management process was well institutionalized. Since first implemented, there had been three changes of command, yet the process continued.

Budget needs for the war in Iraq and Afghanistan resulted in drastic cuts for Army garrisons. Hunter's fiscal year 2006 budget was as astounding 30% below the budget for the prior year. Colonel Hunter attributed the well-oiled cost management process with minimizing the trauma of absorbing the cuts.

Two comments summarize the current state of the process. In the summer of 2006, the official assigned responsibility for designing the Air Force's cost management process visited Fort Huachuca to attend the Garrison Management Review. Afterward he said, "I've dreamt about seeing a meeting like this. Everyone sitting around the table was using cost information logically and constructively to manage the operation." One of the garrison's managers who had witnessed the entire 10-year history of the cost management and control process offered the following, "It is now a way of life and I don't know how we operated without it."

Summary: Conclusions

The garrison at Fort Huachuca built its cost management and control process over a 10-year period. It evolved from an experimental pilot project to an accepted and important part of the operating culture. Over the 10-year period the effort improved operations by providing millions of dollars of resources that were redirected to more critical needs while also improving service quality and avoiding costs of millions more.

Process

The after action review process started on a monthly basis. It evolved to a quarterly process with meetings within the larger directorates occurring before the garrison-wide meeting for the commanding officer.

Early attempts at planning did not take hold. Instead, prior performance filled the requirement of defining expectations. Trended information was used to focus management attention where it was most needed. As noted by the Air Force official, garrison meetings were well done. Participants were obviously prepared. All directorate managers attended and often made helpful comments and suggestions. The meeting was very much one of collaboration.

The meeting's agenda looked at many different aspects of management control. While basically an organization based control process, it brings elements of output into the review process and has looked at some overheads within directorates.

Leadership

Each garrison commander was a strong leader who made the process a success. None had prior experience in cost management. Each changed the process somewhat to emphasize his priorities and in response to his personal style.

Directorate managers have in most cases become good financial managers over the lifetime of the program. Initially, they were probably the biggest barriers to change. This is probably due to their history dealing with budget management and control processes. Change was threatening.

ACE Staff

The analytic cost expert (ACE), Jim Freauff, provided critical support, particularly during the early years. Freauff was the champion of the process, and it is unlikely the effort would have been attempted without his interest.

Initially, he expanded his original job description to include this function. Early successes allowed him to add a couple support people to run all aspects of the measurement process and work with directorate management on research and issues. After a few years, he began working directly for the Garrison Commander in a newly created office. By 2007, the office had four staff and a contractor.

Measurement

The measurement process evolved enormously over the 10-year period. Initially, it was very detailed in spite of Freauff's emphasis on rapid prototyping and short deadlines. For example, the first Logistics Directorate model had 350 cost objects or activities. Subsequent remodeling reduced this to 125 and later to 35. Later additions increased this slightly.

Initially, the measurement effort produced only annual costs. Annual costs offered very little meaningful process input. Early after action reviews required monthly costs, although this was changed to quarterly after the first year. Tools and procedures were developed over time to make the measurement process less burdensome.

The ACE staff worked all the measurement issues with varying degrees of support from existing accounting functions. In fact, relationships with accounting were occasionally adversarial in the early days. It seems that managers researching their costs began to ask questions of accounting practices that exposed some errors and questionable practices. Accounting seems to have improved as a result and has been less of an issue since.

CHAPTER 9

Refocusing Support Functions Through Role Based Control Processes

Introduction

How often should desktop computers be replaced? How many personnel specialists are needed? How long should it take to get a contract issued? Who should have Blackberries?

While these are common questions for support functions, there are few simple or obvious answers. Furthermore, a shared understanding of the issues involved and the tradeoffs implied is unlikely since these issues require expertise typically not found in the core mission functions of the organization.

Managing support functions is challenging, as each support function is usually unique and there are not other functions with which to internally benchmark. Furthermore, most individual support functions do not present a materially large expense category that would warrant extensive involvement from top management. It is easy to conclude that support organizations are more difficult to manage because of their specialized nature, diversity, and number. Yet the total spending on support is often a significant percentage of funding and too important to ignore or leave to chance.

Refocusing support functions can provide greater *efficiency*, freeing resources for core mission functions. But perhaps more importantly, refocusing support functions can significantly improve support's *effectiveness* in its role of enabling the organization's mission.

Significance

Every major organization and many suborganizations have support functions that exist to aid the mainstream core mission, or line, functions of the organization. Support functions typically include facilities, information systems, human resources, accounting, contracting, and security. The important distinction is that, while support functions are critically important, their importance is grounded in the fact that they aid core functions in accomplishing the missions of the organization.

For example, a management information systems organization does not exist solely to provide its own information needs. While it may do so on occasion, its reason for existence is to support the information needs of the rest of the organization.

The cost of support functions is usually significant. Rent and rent related costs are often the second largest source cost (after salary and wages) in federal organizations. Management information systems organizations have also been increasingly expensive given recent efforts to upgrade and expand obsolete systems.

Management Control Issues

Management of support functions, however, often proves to be problematic. Most senior career managers understand the core mission and have demonstrated ability to accomplish that mission over their careers. Few have significant experience in the support areas.

Performance metrics and other measures of success are usually more straightforward and mature for core mission functions. This is not the case for the support areas. Being outside the mainstream, there is often no useful historical or comparison based benchmark for success.

Furthermore, the typical budget process usually does not help. Both the core mission functions and support functions are often funded independently, creating "stovepipes." Each function can begin to feel and act like an independent, self-funded entity. Over time, it is only natural that support stovepipes lose their sense of being support functions. After all, each stovepipe has its own budget just like any core mission function.

The budget independence of support functions creates several frustrations. The first occurs because support is "free" to its consumer.

Independent Stovepipes

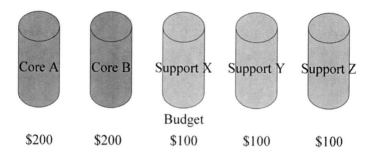

Figure 9.1. Support functions and core functions are often identically funded, making support functions independent stovepipes.

Economists note that "free goods have infinite demand." Logically, core function managers A and B in Figure 9.1 each seek to get as much support as possible from support functions X, Y, and Z. There is no cost to A or B for this support in any financial or budgetary sense.

On the other hand, support functions X, Y, and Z see apparently insatiable demand for their services. Over time, this budget dynamic of insatiable demand for support can easily result in a shift of budget resources from core to support functions. In other words, an organization structure that provides free support to consuming core functions may be doomed to eventual overfunding of that support.

Second, and related to the first frustration, is the likelihood that the core functions are often very poor consumers. "Infinite demand" for "free" services often results in requests for support services that are not rational in an economic sense. Support function managers are often dismayed by consuming organizations that place unreasonable demands for service, technology, or support that would not occur if the consumer/ requester had to pay for them.

The third frustration is that core functions often feel that support functions are nonresponsive. Support functions do not "work" for core functions. While support functions may have large demand for their free services, they often have no organizational motivation or accountability to meet that demand. Note the interesting dynamic: core managers place unreasonably high demands on support functions that have little compelling need to respond.

This in turn leads to the fourth frustration. Core mission function managers believe that their core functions are well managed. They understand their lists of unaffordable and unfunded needs and can resent the support organizations, which may be seen as unnecessarily large, growing, and unresponsive. Organizational tension can become very high when budgets are tightened.

The resulting situation is that an organization structure and management process that isolates one from the other often frustrates both core mission and support function managers. Both are insulated from the positive economic impact of knowing the cost of support, of buying the appropriate level, and of continuously working to improve the efficiency of support in provision and consumption. Fixing these frustrations requires a two-pronged approach that refocuses support. First, the approach must change the economic relationship so that consumers of support "pay" for their consumption, and second, the approach must create a process or forum for interaction that enables and encourages continuous improvement in the ability of support to further the organization's mission. This implies a fundamental consensus that the role of support is to support line functions.

Refocusing the Economics of Support Functions

Refocusing the economics of support functions requires a mechanism for costing the consumption of their services. Several alternatives exist. Internal service funds and revolving funds, for example, may charge for goods or services on a transaction by transaction basis. Alternatively, allocation of support costs is a much less expensive process and may be the only practical costing method when support is not consumed on a transaction basis. The costing mechanics must exhibit the following three attributes in order to facilitate refocusing support function.

First, the distribution of support cost to core mission functions must be useful in expressing and exposing the economics of consumption and motivating desired behavior. The core function that uses fewer facilities, for example, should receive a lower allocation of facilities' cost. In other words, the cost of support to the core function should reflect its consumption on a cause-and-effect basis.

This means that the choice of allocation basis is important. For example, facilities cost distributed to consumers on the basis of their full-time employees may not represent consumption if some consumers require more square footage per employee or more expensive square footage than others do. Furthermore, such an allocation practice may encourage an increase in square footage per employee over time.

Second, the distribution of support cost must be credible. Credibility is essential if managers are expected to use it to make decisions and behavior changes.

Unfortunately, some allocation software is so difficult to understand that it becomes unexplainable in any practical sense. It becomes a "black box" that produces numbers for which managers will not accept accountability or trust for decision making.

Third, the process of cost distribution must be affordable. There is theoretically no limit to the detail (and the resulting cost of processing that detail) that can be incurred in costing. However, rapidly diminishing returns to effort argue for simple, straightforward, inexpensive costing. This argument is particularly strong during start-up of the refocusing process.

For purposes of this chapter, consider that the cost distribution process yields the following matrix from the original example. The matrix presents the organization shown in Figure 9.1 in an entirely different light.

Consider the situation depicted in Table 9.1. Costs from the support functions are allocated or charged in a manner that shows the total responsibility costs of the core functions. Managers of A and B are now in the position to weigh the relative value to their operations of support functions X, Y, and Z. Furthermore, core managers A and B are now in a position to make tradeoffs between support costs and additions or

Table 9.1

	Core A	Core B	Total
Owned Costs	200	200	400
Allocated from Support X	10	90	100
Allocated from Support Y	50	50	100
Allocated from Support Z	60	40	100
Total Responsibility Cost	320	380	700

reductions in their owned costs. Support managers X, Y, and Z can now see their roles in the organization's core missions.

Virtual Organization Chart: The Cost Chain of Command

Allocating support cost to its consumers effectively creates a virtual organization chart (Figure 9.2) that provides a different view of the "cost chain of command." Core managers can now be accountable for the "full" costs of their operations. Note that support functions are clearly recognized as part of the core functions in the cost chain of command.

Allocating support costs to their consuming line functions changes the management dynamics in a number of useful ways. First, support managers find themselves explaining results and costs to core function managers as well as answering to the general manager. Second, core function managers now have a clear view of "full cost" in their functions and must be able to explain their consumption of support resources to the general manager.

Cost Chain of Command

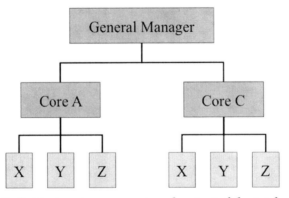

Figure 9.2. Support costs are now viewed as part of the total cost of core functions rather than as independent stovepipes.

It is even possible to provide budget to support organizations through the line functions. In other words, core functions A and B could be budgeted at $320 and $380 as in Table 9.1. A and B could then pay for their consumption of support functions X, Y, and Z. The support functions are therefore effectively financed as an internal service fund or revolving fund, receiving no direct appropriation.

Refocusing Support Function Interactions

Simply costing out support consumption and even adding dotted lines to an organization chart are unlikely to really change much on their own. A role based leadership driven management control process is necessary to change behavior in ways that drive continuous improvement in mission support. This process calls for a periodic meeting—that is, interaction between managers accountable for change.

The support after action review calls for principals from support functions to present to principals from the core functions and the general manager. The presentation contains cost and performance information. Besides conveying basic resource information, the support cost after action review provides a needed forum for interaction.

The organization's general manager convenes the support after action review and schedules principals from support functions to present to principals from the core mission functions. Support function managers must present their costs and accomplishments of the period and their allocations to each of the core mission functions.

Most importantly, support managers are also expected to explain their results. Explanations can be done in comparison to planned expectations, in comparison to historical trends, or both. These explanations compel support managers to research and learn about the financial dimensions of their operations and show core function consumers the financial aspects of their consumption.

The meeting also provides an opportunity for support managers to discuss their specific continuous improvement initiatives. They should be expected to present their tactical and strategic initiatives. This requirement assumes that such initiatives are under way and active.

Core function managers should be active participants in the support after action review. They should ask questions, make suggestions, and request follow-up actions and analyses as appropriate. The organization head should also take an active role in the meeting to ensure that constructive interaction occurs while signaling the importance of continuous improvement, efficient support, and rational consumption.

The outcomes from a successful after action review should be increased understanding for all participants, action items requiring follow-up work, and decisions to be implemented.

Information Requirements

Quarterly, or perhaps even monthly, cost data from support functions are essential. Performance data are also desirable. The costing methodology must be approved by all consuming core functions as fair and logical. Usually, this means a consumption based measurement process.[1]

Allocation is probably the most used costing methodology to associate support costs with the core functions they support. There are three different conceptual frameworks for the cost allocation process. First, the easiest and most understandable allocation process is "direct, simple" allocation. This process handles each support function separately and seeks a distribution basis (such as the number of employees, square footage occupied, or management estimates of effort) to allocate cost simply and directly to the core functions.

Direct Simple Allocation

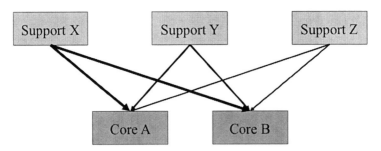

Figure 9.3. Direct, simple allocation takes all support cost directly to core function consumers.

Figure 9.3 shows a direct, simple allocation process. Each support function is allocated directly to its ultimate, core function consumer.

Criticism of direct, simple allocation notes that consumption of support functions is not limited to core functions. The human resources department processes personnel actions for the accounting department. The accounting department provides paychecks for the human resources department staff. It is possible that almost every support function provides some support for every other support function. Accounting for all these interactions is extremely complex and is generally done through some sort of "reciprocal" allocation methodology.

Second, Figure 9.4 shows the paths inherent in a reciprocal cost allocation model for the same situation. Note that while direct, simple allocation has a total of 6 paths, reciprocal allocation has a total of 15 paths. Note also that reciprocal allocation even considers the allocation of each support function to itself! (Accounting processes payroll for accounting.)

Allocation software packages usually process this type of allocation iteratively. That is, an allocation is made that results in perhaps 10% of the cost still left in support functions. The second allocation iteration would result in 1% (10% of 10%) still left in support functions. The process continues to iterate until some small fraction of a dollar remains in support functions. Although this may not sound overly complex, some large models take all night to complete the iterative process.

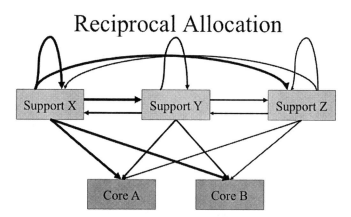

Reciprocal Allocation

Figure 9.4. Reciprocal allocations attempts to account for all possible consumption paths although all cost ultimately ends in the core functions.

Reciprocal allocations attempt to capture all elements of support consumption. While more precise, reciprocal mechanics are unarguably much more difficult to understand and explain, often masking other, more serious, costing flaws.

The third common allocation methodology is a compromise between the ease of direct, simple allocation and the comprehensiveness of reciprocal allocation. "Step down" allocation recognizes that some support-to-support interactions are important to capture while most are not material.

Step down allocation works by establishing a hierarchy of support functions ranked by the materiality of their support-to-support interactions. For example, a facility cost related support function may have the most material consumption of its support used by other support functions (everyone uses space). The facilities cost would then be distributed to core functions and all support functions.

If, for example, the management information systems department were the second most material function, it would be allocated in the next "step" down the hierarchy. Its cost would be distributed to all core functions and the remaining support functions on lower steps but not to facilities. Support-to-support allocations would continue until all steps were completed or it would stop at any point and revert to a direct, simple approach for remaining support functions.

Step Down Allocation

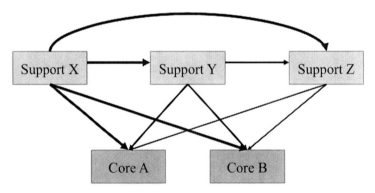

Figure 9.5. Step down allocation recognizes some support-to-support consumption in the process of moving all cost to core functions.

Figure 9.5 illustrates the step down process in the three support function, two core function example. Support X allocates to Core A, Core B, Support Y, and Support Z. The second step sees Support Y allocated to Core A, Core B, and Support Z. The final step has Support Z allocated to Core A and Core B. Note that 9 paths of cost exist in this model compared to the 6 in direct, simple and the 15 in reciprocal allocation.

All three allocation methodologies are similar in that initially cost resides in both support and core functions and that ultimately all cost resides in core functions. The difference is the number of pathways by which cost migrates to core functions.

Step down allocation presents a very reasonable approach that captures important consumption relationships while not detracting from credibility through the complexity of reciprocal allocation. Managers who receive allocated cost via a reciprocal process find it too easy to question or reject numbers that nobody can clearly explain. On the other hand, direct, simple allocation may miss important consumption and encourage undesirable behaviors. Consider, for example, the negative impact of allocating the facilities department on a direct, simple basis. It is very possible that core functions would be motivated to reduce the space they occupy but that support functions would move into that space because it was "free." Clearly, this would be an undesirable outcome.

Barriers to Success

The greatest barriers to success are cultural and represent a natural resistance to change. Support managers may fear exposure of the details of their operations. Core function managers may likewise fear exposure of their support consumption. The underlying fear is typically a resistance to accountability.

Resistance is manifested in a several ways. Calls for lots of detailed cost backup to allocations can make the measurement process extremely expensive, prohibitively time consuming, and actually more difficult to understand. Another common claim is that the cost is fixed and that trying to manage fixed cost is wasteful. Furthermore, the argument is often made that improving efficiency results in lower budgets in future years, as if this argument is somehow in the long-term interest of the organization.

Another objection is the argument that support cost should also be distributed to other support functions. This argument has some traction and deserves considerable attention. As discussed earlier, it may make sense to consider a few support functions, such as facilities and management information systems, and distribute them through a step down methodology.

Some Practical Applications

A few years ago the Federal Deposit Insurance Corporation found a mismatch in the ratio of support cost to line cost. Both core and support functions had been increased years earlier to support the Banking Resolution Trust. Over time, core functions in banking supervision and in the disposition of failed banks gradually drew down their staffing levels. Support functions, however, did not reduce their size correspondingly.

The research and development laboratory of the United States Navy located in San Diego, California, had a similar problem in the mid-1990s. The commanding officer believed that high costs of support functions were making the lab noncompetitive. Both organizations initiated role based control processes to increase their cost effectiveness. The Navy effort is described extensively in chapter 10.

On a bigger scale, the entire Navy is looking at its core enterprises and the relationship of support with those enterprises. Chief of Naval Operations Admiral Gary Roughead stated, "It's about collaborating, sharing, and enhancing our business practices. Not to turn the Navy into a business, but to understand the business of the Navy so that we remain the most effective and efficient Navy in the world."[2]

The Navy created the Navy Enterprise effort in recognition of the need for a "revolution in business affairs." The Navy's cost chain of command recognizes five major warfare product lines (*enterprises* to use their terminology): surface warfare, naval aviation, undersea warfare, expeditionary combat, and network warfare. The goals of Navy Enterprise are described as follows:

NAVY Enterprise is an initiative designed to improve the understanding of our business practices so we remain the most effective and efficient Navy in the world. Our resources—people, time, and money—are precious and we must ensure we are maximizing our Return on Investment (ROI) in all we do. Our workforce—active duty, reservist, and civilian—is our most valuable resource. They are improving the way we do business every day by focusing on the warfighter and promoting an open and collaborative culture committed to delivering current readiness and future capability requirements needed to accomplish the mission.

Our two key methods to improve ROI are:

- *Improving the output/cost ratio associated with all major processes*
- *Aligning and resourcing our lines of business to achieve the intended outcome in the most effective and efficient manner*[3]

Periodic reviews by senior leaders have two major sections. One seeks to "baseline the domain" through detailing each entity's staffing, budget, equipment, and role. The second section calls for "maximizing current and future value." This section gets to the heart of the "governance" process and calls for detailed explanations of each support function's leadership process for continuous improvement, framework for innovation, and examples of productivity initiatives. These requirements include not only the entity efforts but the efforts of its key contractors as well.

Conclusions

Refocusing indirect support functions through role based control should be relatively simpler to implement than organization based or output based control processes because it involves fewer people and a simpler, more centralized view of cost. The process requires a support after action review that can be supported with highly aggregated cost information that should be relatively easy to acquire in most organizations. Some allocation methodology is required, but that need not be obsessively detailed.

Refocusing support costs has two requirements. First, support functions must be viewed differently in an economic sense. Support costs must be reasonably determined for each core consumer. Those costs can be budgeted, charged, or allocated operationally to create a virtual cost chain of command. Either way, the key is to create a provider-consumer relationship while providing core managers with a view of the "full cost" of their responsibilities.

Second, support functions must have an institutionalized forum of interaction with their customers. This is the primary purpose of the support after action review. The idea is to get principal providers and consumers together periodically in a meeting where support managers present to the core functions managers. Such interaction reinforces the supplier-customer relationship while creating the opportunity for leaders and managers to drive continuous improvement in the support function.

Refocusing indirect support functions may be the lowest cost to implement, highest return on investment management opportunity for most government organizations. The process creates value by improving the linkage between support functions and their customers in ways that promote accountability and enable continuous improvement in efficiency.

CHAPTER 10

NRaD (Now SPAWAR Systems Center Pacific)

Case Study

Introduction

The Navy R&D Center San Diego is now known as Space and Naval Warfare Systems Center Pacific (SSC Pacific). It is the U.S. Navy's research, development, test and evaluation, engineering, and fleet support center for command, control, and communication systems, and ocean surveillance. It occupies a portion of the Point Loma peninsula in San Diego.

SSC Pacific was established June 1, 1940, as the Navy's first West Coast laboratory. Today, the Center spends roughly $1.8 billion per year and employs more than 3,800 civilian and military personnel, the majority of them engineers, scientists, and technicians. SSC Pacific is responsible for developing technology to collect, transmit, process, display, and, most critically, manage information essential for successful military operations. The Center develops the capabilities that allow decision makers of the Navy and, increasingly, of the joint services to carry out their operational missions and protect their forces.

Information—financial, administrative, statistical, technical—is the lifeblood of the modern world. For the U.S. Navy's tactical commanders at sea, information can well mean the difference between victory and defeat, life and death.

Our business is C4ISR—Command, Control, Communications, Computers, Intelligence, Surveillance, Reconnaissance—providing the information technology resources essential to the U.S. warfighter in today's increasingly complex, increasingly hostile world. In the development of these technologies, we are contributing substantially to the achievement of the future vision of the Department of Defense and particularly of the U.S. Navy. Forcefully stated in the Sea Power 21 concept of the Chief of Naval Operations, this vision centers on sea-based operations using "revolutionary information superiority and dispersed, networked force capabilities to deliver unprecedented offensive power, defensive assurance, and operational independence to Joint Force Commanders."[1]

The research and development facility is led by a Navy captain, while the staff includes many scientists and engineers and is primarily civilian. The stimulus for the Overhead Review process came from the Commanding Officer, Captain Kirk Evans. He had been exposed to activity based cost accounting and hoped that a study would offer some insights into overhead distribution. It was not initially anticipated that the study would lead to an Overhead Review process that has lasted more than 15 years.

Call to Action—The First Overhead Review Meeting

Look gentlemen, the bottom line is that we have to get our costs down. I know of only two ways to do this. One is the Soviet Method and that means Central Planning. I can get a can of paint tonight and put black X's on buildings I want you out of. And you will get out!

The other way is the Free Enterprise Method. Costing will show you what things really cost and then I will look to you as good officers, government employees and Americans to do the right thing . . . Which Method do you want?

Captain Kirk Evans
Commanding Officer, 1994
Navy R&D Center, San Diego

This statement from the Commanding Officer occurred at the first Overhead Review some 15 years ago. The agenda for the meeting had the managers of the overhead support functions proposing new allocation mechanisms and showing resulting cost distributions to their customers, the research division managers.

The stimulus to Captain Evans's outburst was the vocal opposition of two of the research division managers to the proposed distribution of $17.3 million facilities costs. Previously, this cost had been distributed on the cost basis of labor dollars spent by each division. This meant that, for example, a division that had 20% of the Center's R&D labor received an allocated cost of 20% of the Center's facilities expense. See Figure 10.1 for the actual allocations based on labor and on the proposed method.

The proposed method used a different basis of cost distribution: square footage occupied. This meant a division that occupied 20% of buildings would receive a cost allocation for facilities of 20% of the Center's facilities expense regardless of how many people it had. Needless to say, the vocal objections to the new methodology came from Division 50 and Division 80 managers: those whose allocations would increase. Implicitly, then, those divisions enjoyed more space per capita than other divisions whose cost allocations would decline.[2]

Space limitations had been a chronic problem at the Center for decades. Temporary buildings built during World War II were still being used 50 years after the war ended. Growing R&D divisions (Division 40) whose services were most in demand were crammed into tight spaces while divisions whose work was declining (Division 50) seemed to never relinquish space.

The cost distribution made a difference to the research divisions. They did not receive appropriations to fund their work. Instead, they received what amounted to "grants" or contracts for specific work needed by other Naval Commands and Department of Defense organizations. Facility expense changes would eventually become part of the cost rate embedded

R & D Div	30	40	50	70	80	Total
Labor basis	2.3	5.1	2.4	3.8	3.7	$17.3M
Footage basis	.0	4.0	4.6	4.1	4.6	$17.3M
Change	2.3	1.1	(2.2)	(.3)	(.9)	–

Figure 10.1. Cost allocations for site facilities costs to research divisions.

in their bids for new work. Increased costs could make them less competitive, while decreased cost could make them more competitive.

Yet those division managers who would benefit from the proposed change in facilities expense distribution remained quiet. Those with allocation increases raised a number of objections:

1. "Facility expense is a fixed cost. Fixed costs don't change, so why bother."
2. "I won't pay bills that aren't stated to the penny. This is only a gross approximation of my bill."
3. "My space isn't as new or nice as other space. The square footage allocation assumes each square foot causes exactly the same amount of facilities expense."

Captain Evans's offer of a choice of method brought discussion to a close. Nobody wanted him out painting that night, and an agreement was reached to try the proposed allocation basis. The Controller found it very easy to include a line in every cost center's monthly report that included a cost labeled "facility expense" based on that cost center's square footage occupied.

The next day divisions began turning in space that "they no longer needed." In the first year, this totaled 35,000 square feet. Certain buildings no longer needed janitorial services or heating and cooling. This was also true for some floors in other buildings. Freed-up space also allowed people to move out of the World War II Quonset huts, allowing those high-maintenance buildings to be demolished.

The next year's annual report showed direct savings from this action as more than a million dollars with a similar amount avoided.

Leadership Driven Management

Resistance to change was significant. Clearly, this change would not have occurred without Captain Evans's leadership. He initiated the study in the first place as part of his mission to make the lab more competitive. This began with training on the principles of managerial costing. More importantly, he overrode the opposition to change that occurs especially when accountability relationships are involved.

The period of opposition proved to be short lived. Leaders from research and support functions both quickly grasped the benefits of their new "cost intelligence." They became responsible for its use.

Captain Evans soon left the position of Commanding Officer of the Center as military commanders inevitably do. Subsequent commanding officers and managers continued the Overhead Review Meeting. It has continued on a monthly basis for more than 15 years and has even expanded in scope.

Process: The Overhead Review Meeting

The Overhead Review survived and flourished because it added value far beyond its cost. It addressed the interface between line and staff functions and created a forum for interaction that provides benefits to both.

Previously, overhead functions often seemed isolated from the cost and performance pressures that typically fell to the line research divisions struggling to get work and complete it within budget.

Now it seems that the Overhead Review created a forum for interaction between overhead functions and their customers that is valuable even in the absence of dramatic improvements such as those that followed the first meeting. Support organizations have become cost managed organizations. It is likely that the Review provides value to both the overhead provided and the overhead consumer.

Eliminated Free Goods

"Free goods" have infinite demand, and consumption of overhead had never before been associated with cost. When overhead support is free, or appears free, it is not surprising that line functions want all they can get. Moreover, it could be expected that core function organizations would see unrealistic "needs" for personal computers, laptops, blackberries, and so forth. This is often frustrating to support providers.

Cost Informed Demand for Overhead

When line functions "pay" for support, it is likely that "needs" become more realistic and focused. Paying for what you get means you get what you pay for. Research divisions, the overhead consumer, have likely become better consumers. Yes, more space, for example, may be available, but it will never be free. A request for more space now implies the need to do a cost benefit tradeoff.

Previously, the size of space occupied did not have this cost linkage. The facilities allocation based on labor dollars was essentially a payroll tax. Perhaps it could influence staffing decisions, but it certainly had no impact on requests for space and facilities support.[3] Previously, "free" space now came with a rent bill, and rational consumers changed their behavior almost instantly.

More Empowered Line Functions

Research division managers' scope of authority increases as they influence overhead functions in and through the Overhead Review. Simply, the recognition that line functions are the customer, the ultimate source of overhead funding, has impact on support function behavior.

As the research division managers came to understand that they were the bill payers for support, they became much more interested in what was happening in support areas. The Overhead Review Meeting became a monthly institution because it gave insight into what was happening. Issues could be discussed and decisions reached because all the bill payers were in the room.

More Effective Support Functions

Support managers also found that their customers became less demanding and critical. The research division managers became less demanding because now they only demanded what they were willing to pay for. Demands truly became "needs" rather than "wishes." The research managers became less critical because over time they came to understand the costs, problems, limitations, and concerns of the support managers.

The Overhead Review Meeting involved almost all the leaders in the organization. Support managers, usually with a lower job grade than their customers, had the undivided attention of the Center's most senior executives. The Commanding Officer and the Technical Director—the highest level civilian employee—attended, as did other key people including the Controller.

Better Costing

Lastly, it should be clear that the "true, underlying, real cost" of the research divisions became more accurate. Support cost is often significant and allocation that is not based on consumption invariably sees some line functions subsidizing others.

In this case, a clear picture developed that Division 50 was being systematically subsidized in many ways. This understanding led to significant rethinking of its strategy and its role within the Center. Subsequently, this led to reorganization and elimination of its least cost effective elements.

Staff

No additional staff was required. Several personnel had been trained in managerial costing. The initial effort required 20 or 30 days of consultant time to work with support managers in determining how to reasonably reflect the consumption of their resources by the research divisions.

Overhead costs are generally known in aggregate. Allocation processes need not require great staff efforts. In fact, it is likely that simple, easy-to-implement processes are the easiest to understand. Such credibility is an important prerequisite to the behavioral changes seen in this study.

Cost Measurement

All cost information needed was readily available in existing accounting systems. None were added or modified. Allocations mechanics were kept simple enough that only Excel was needed. Even the most complex support function was distributed with only a handful of allocations.

Part of the agenda for the first Overhead Review Meeting was to gain consensus of all research divisions regarding the appropriateness of the cost distribution methodology. The only stipulation was that the method had to reasonably reflect consumption of the support function's resources.

Precision (with its own inherent cost) of cost measurement was not the goal. The goal was credibility and managerial usefulness at low cost. This raised a couple issues where precision was deliberately forgone.

Distribution of the cost of the Patent Support Office was one of those areas. Cost was reasonably reflected by the number of patent requests submitted. However, it was felt that allocating on that basis would discourage patent applications, which was not in the organization's best interest. It was therefore decided to allocate this cost like a tax, but only on the scientists and engineers. This method essentially "prepaid" for patent support and motivated research divisions to get their fair share.

Hazardous waste disposal was another interesting area. Cost could be precisely distributed based on the way disposal was paid for dollars per pound submitted. However, this would motivate bad practices of disposal avoidance and infinite storage. It was decided to allocate on the basis of pounds of hazardous material in inventory, thus discouraging excessive inventory and providing real advantages to finding nonhazardous substitutes.

Another important area of allocation technique came up when reviewing the facility allocations shown in Figure 10.1 with Captain Evans, the commanding officer. He was concerned that allocating all facilities cost directly to the research division might have an unintended consequence.

While research divisions would certainly become cost sensitive, there was a danger that other organizations in support roles would not have the same motivations. It would be quite likely that line functions would vacate space they did not need, and support functions would move into that space because it was "free" to them. Such a result would create morale issues and significantly reduce the benefits.

A partial application of step down allocation was the solution to this management issue. Facilities cost was allocated first to all organizations on site—that is, line research divisions and support functions. Everybody came to see facilities as a line in their own cost report. Other support functions would include their facility allocation as part of their own cost in subsequent allocations to research divisions.

The ultimate distribution of facilities to research divisions probably did not change significantly from Figure 10.1 Most of the cost would come directly from facilities as part of the first step. The rest would be embedded in the allocations from the other support functions on site.

Knowing the ultimate distribution of facilities by research division was unimportant. Providing all organizations with "rent" cost was important and was achieved by this one step allocation process.[4]

An Allocation Methodology Example: Safety and Environment

The approach to allocation used may have significantly influenced the acceptance and institutionalization of the Overhead Review Meeting. Perhaps it is worth looking at one in detail.

The Safety and Environmental Office spent $1.5 million per year and had roughly 50 studies, tasks, inspections, reports, and responsibilities. The manager, not surprisingly, wanted initially to develop allocations for each of these "activities." Discussion, however, resulted in three groupings of work product.

One group was 23 work activities related to facilities and buildings (shown in Figure 10.2). A second group was made around the work related to hazardous materials. The third group covered the small number of remaining miscellaneous functions.

The cost of each of the three groupings was estimated based on work assignments and time reporting. The building related group was allocated based on square footage. The hazardous material related group was allocated based on pounds of hazardous materials in inventory, and the miscellaneous group on a factor that combined the number of people trained, items of safety equipment issued, number of exams, and net square footage.

Table 10.1 shows the resulting distribution in comparison to the previously used labor based method.

This allocation process exposed new insights into overhead consumption. Not only was Division 50 being subsidized, but it showed that tenant organizations were getting truly "free goods." This and other overhead allocations showed that tenant organizations received the benefit of roughly a million dollars per year in support services without paying for them. Subsequent changes in the Internal Service Agreements corrected this. The allocation documents provided all the proof needed to recover these funds to the Navy R&D Center.

Site Wide Facilities and Buildings "Components"

- Water Pollution Prevention Program
- Asbestos Management
- Solid Waste Management
- Installation Restoration Program
- RADON Program
- Emergency Management Program
- Drinking Water Program
- UST Program (Removal)
- Energy Control (Lock out/tagout)
- Emergency Radiation Program
- Reports of Unsafe Conditions
- Confined Space Entry Program

- Air Pollution Prevention Program
- Ride-Share Program
- Ozone Depletion Management
- Morris Dam, La Posta, Sentinel AZ.
- Pre-Construction Meetings/Plan Reviews
- Environmental Compliance Evaluations
- NAVOSH Abatement Program
- Lead Management Program
- PCB Management
- Hearing Conservation/Noise Abatement
- Indoor Air Quality

Figure 10.2. Some of the activities of the Safety and Environmental Office.

Table. 10.1. Allocation Comparison—Safety and Environmental Office

R&D Div	Other	30	40	50	70	80	Tenants	Total
Original Basis ($K)	26	175	405	249	305	302	0	1,462
Proposed Basis ($K)	0	25	141	609	203	240	244	1,462
Change ($K)	26	150	264	(360)	102	62	(244)	0

Conclusion

Mike McDonough, a systems engineer in one of the research divisions, recently conducted a site-sponsored review of the Overhead Review Meeting as part of his MBA thesis. His review indicated that the Overhead Review Meeting is a process that is still very much alive and evolving. His summary is shown in Exhibit 1.

Research Division Managers thought the meeting to be significant for a couple reasons. First, they saw it as a strategic opportunity to get insight and direction from site leadership. Second, they saw the meeting as an opportunity to share their overhead management experiences with their peers while also learning from them. The key to this learning was undoubtedly the environment senior leaders supported: the goal was to aid in accomplishing the mission rather than extracting retribution.

Cathy McLane, SSC Pacific's Controller, believes the Overhead Review was institutionalized because

> this process is a forum for gaining awareness of Center financial activities and business processes and it is a conduit for knowledge transfer and sharing of best business practices in financial management across the Departments/Stakeholders. It quietly (or unintentionally) stimulates learning for future leaders and continuous improvement.

This case shows a very high return on investment. Hundreds, perhaps thousands, of similar opportunities must exist.

EXHIBIT

Overhead Review Synopsis

A Summary of the SSC Pacific Overhead Review, Its Purpose, Roles, and Expectations

Michael McDonough
January 19, 2009

Introduction

Intended Audience

The intended audience for this paper is the center technical director, the deputy for operations, the controller, department heads and their resource managers, as well as division heads and their resource managers. Additionally, employees interested in understanding how the center overhead is financially and strategically managed may find this document helpful.

Background

This study was initiated by the comptroller's office in an effort to improve the current center Overhead Review and financial indicators meeting. Observations made during meeting attendance were paired with interviews conducted with leadership across the center to gain a better understanding of the intended purpose of the review and what it accomplishes in its current state.

Objective

This document establishes standard expectations for the Overhead Review and indicators meeting. It should be used as a training document as well as a baseline for growth and improvement.

Scope

This document is based on interviews with the attendees of the Overhead Review Meeting and observation of the meeting from January through June 2008.

Review Purpose

Financial Awareness

The center Overhead Review and financial indicators meeting provides an opportunity for the center's financial state to be socialized among the center leadership. The comptroller and the technical director receive budgetary information from headquarters and funding sources that influences center policy. This information must flow out to department heads and their resource managers. The intent is to empower the departments to make strategic decisions with the center's financial state in mind.

Measurement

The center Overhead Review and financial indicators meeting is the venue for reporting financial data collected by the comptroller. Because the comptroller provides look-ahead slides to the technical director and the data are also held by the departments, all parties at the meeting should already know what the data show. The meeting, therefore, provides an opportunity for the outstanding positive and negative data to be discussed. This discussion is critical for leadership to learn and improve. It can be difficult to discuss challenges or issues in a group setting, but this information is valuable, and the environment supports solutions and not criticism. The group provides the opportunity to discuss what contributes to good and bad situations that may be similar across departments. This discussion is imperative for the continuous improvement of center leadership.

Training

The center Overhead Review and financial indicators meeting is also a training tool. Division heads and resource managers are encouraged to attend in order to be prepared for the next step in their careers. Understanding the responsibilities of their superiors can broaden the abilities of employees.

Roles and Responsibilities

Center Level Strategic Planner

This role is defined by those who make decisions for the center as a whole. This includes the Technical Director, the Deputy for Operations and the Comptroller. The primary responsibility of this group is to analyze the financial data presented at the meeting. "Strategic decision making" means directing and empowering the next tier of employees, so these become additional responsibilities of the group. It is expected that this group will be familiar with the presentation of the data enough to ask questions and prompt discussion on important points.

Center Level Financial Information Provider

This group collects and supplies data for the use of the review attendees. This role is filled by the Comptroller's office. This group is responsible for providing objective and accurate center financial data. They also lead the meeting by briefing slides to the attendees.

Department Data Owner

This group includes those that are accountable for their department's portion of the provided financial data. Department heads and department resource managers both fit into this role. This group is responsible for explaining to the Center Level Strategic Planners any deviations from projections and addressing any additional questions. It is expected that the department data owners have in-depth knowledge of the finances of the department. This is necessary to explain to the attendees what they do to achieve excellent results or what problems they face so the attendees can help to solve them.

Intended Outcome

To become a center that takes the following actions:

- Budgets accurately
- Recognizes out-of-control processes
- Positively reacts to issues
- Makes strategic decisions based on high financial awareness and understanding

CHAPTER 11

Output Based Management Control

Many government organizations are mass producers of something. That is to say, they provide a service or product that is fairly uniform. Social Security processes claims. The Food and Drug Administration reviews applications for new drugs. The Patent and Trademark Office reviews new inventions. In such situations, it is possible to develop a management control process focused or based on outputs.

Outputs are often important enough that some government entities are organized around those outputs. In this sense, the output based control process is similar to previously discussed organization based control processes. There are, however, some important differences.

The most important difference is that measuring the costs of outputs is significantly more complex than measuring organization costs only. This is because the cost of outputs is usually a "full" cost. That is, the cost includes all relevant costs in the production or provision of the output.

This means that indirect costs and overheads must be allocated. This is similar to measurements used in the previously discussed role based control. However, in this case, support costs are allocated to different types of outputs rather than different organizations.

It is also possible that a matrix-type organization exists in which a manager has output responsibility but does not manage any of the organization elements that produce the outputs. Furthermore, some organizations with well-defined outputs have not designated managers with specific responsibilities for outputs. In both cases, the measurement process is further complicated by the need for mechanisms to allocate or distribute direct costs in addition to indirect and support costs.

Manufacturing like outputs will also include costs for materials that are not reviewed in the organization based control process. These are often large, and their materiality suggests that they be paid significant management attention.

Another distinction common to government organizations with well-defined outputs is the possibility of user fees that totally or partially cover their cost of operations. It is sometimes the case in user fee situations that the paying customer is an active participant in the cost review and management control process.

Furthermore, it is likely that the costing will be useful in the fee setting process. This is likely because of a truth based congruence. Managerial costing seeks to understand the true cost of operations, and user fees strongly grounded in costs are often sought because they are easy to defend.

The Output Based Control Process

The basic process in output based control is identical to those previously discussed. The goal is to stimulate performance improvement by reviewing recent performance and planned improvement efforts. The process includes elements of organization based improvement as well as the elements of indirect support improvement.

The major distinction is the broader scope of the review. For example, the fullness nature of the cost will focus management attention on areas of greatest materiality. It is also possible that organizations funded entirely with user fees will want to look at the residual or profit numbers obtained by subtracting cost from fees for each output.

Another option is to focus on measures of unit cost. Such a measure divides output cost by output volume and may be an important metric.

Simple Output Cost Views

The simplest output based control processes would focus only on the cost elements that would include direct and indirect costs. Direct costs are those most closely associated with the product or service. Direct labor and direct materials are commonly measured for manufactured products. Indirect costs include support costs, overheads, and any other costs not included in the direct category.

Simple Cost Results and Reconciliation

Output A	Plan or Prior	Actual	Delta
Direct Cost			
Indirect Cost			
Total Cost			X

Reconciliation Explanation for Delta for Output A

Reason 1: Change in Number of Units	
Reason 2: Change in Direct Cost	
Reason 3: Change in Indirect Cost	
Total Cost Explained	X

Figure 11.1. Output based after action reviews are complicated by the fact that a change in output can drive a change in cost.

Figure 11.1 shows the simplest possible view. Note that the first thing that is different about an output based review is that change in output level is a likely explanatory variable. A higher volume of output should result in higher cost level and this fact says nothing about cost effectiveness in performance.[1]

It is probable that the format actually used in after action reviews would include several key elements of direct and indirect costs based on their materiality or volatility. Figure 11.1 also shows the lowest level of aggregation possible: an individual output. It is possible that a hierarchical approach could be implemented with higher level reviews occurring. For example, an output manager responsible for outputs A, B, and C might review the performance embedded in the figure while aggregating costs for all three outputs to present to a higher level output manager responsible for outputs A, B, C, D, E, and F.

The focus of the after action review is to explain the "delta," or variance, from expectation shown as "X" in Figure 11.1. There are usually a few significant factors that explain most of any delta. The trivial many need not be explained.

Deltas in output based control processes often find explanatory value in studying the impact of change in units from expectation to actual.

Variance analysis in cost accounting texts labels this as a volume variance. Technically, it can be calculated by restating actual costs that would have been expected had the expected volume or number of units been equal to the actual.

For example, consider an operation with a fixed rent of $100 and an expected variable cost per unit of $10. If the plan was to produce 50 units, the cost plan would have been $100 plus $500 (50 units times $10 per unit) for a total of $600. Now, what if we produced 60 units and total cost went up to $650? Note that the total variance is ($50): $50 unfavorable, since cost increased $50.

Variance analysis would recalculate the expected cost with the actual number of units. This equals $100 plus $600 (60 units times $10 per unit) for a total of $700. The difference between the $700 and the originally expected $600 is labeled as volume variance and in this example would be expressed as ($100), unfavorable $100. The difference between $700 and the actual cost of $650 is labeled as performance variance. In this example, performance variance is $50, favorable $50. Note that the ($100) and the $50 net to the total variance of ($50).

The reconciliation explanation of this performance would note that costs increased $100 due to the 20% increase in output. It would also note that improved performance saved $50 due to performance improvements that lowered the average cost per unit.

Profit and Loss Views

Organizations charging user fees are logical candidates for profit and loss views of operations. User fees represent revenues and subtracting costs yields a residual. That residual is roughly equivalent to profit. Some user fee statutes place limits on the residual in terms of a plus or minus. Some accumulate residuals as a reserve. User fee pricing changes are triggered when the reserve increases or falls to prescribed levels or the plus or minus exceeds limits.

These organizations are likely to benefit from an output based control process that stresses the profit and loss view. Building this view requires determination of the direct and indirect costs of each output. The after action review process would use a profit and loss type statement. Explanations of performance would center on a reconciliation statement that would research and report the reasons for differences in planned and actual performance. (See Figure 11.2.)

As in the simple cost view, this view supports further detail as desired and enables aggregation to support hierarchical management approaches. Note also that volume and performance variance opportunities again apply. In fact, volume variance will also have a revenue component. For example, the case used to illustrate variance in the simple view would typically see favorable volume variance for increased units. This occurs because more volume brings in more revenue that more than offsets the unfavorable cost volume variance. (This is the case unless variable cost per unit cost exceeds unit price.)

Other variances are possible in complex cases. For example, there are techniques to analyze pricing variances and to break down performance variance into spending and efficiency components. Even more variance analysis is possible when fixed costs are important. Actual implementations and use of many of the possible variances are probably lower than implied in cost accounting texts. As a practical matter, their value is limited if managers cannot explain or understand their meaning. The relatively simple volume and performance variances discussed here should suffice in most cases.

P&L View Results and Reconciliation

Output A	Plan or Prior	Actual	Delta
Fee Revenue			
Cost			
Residual			X

Reconciliation Explanation for Delta for Residual

Reason 1: Change in Revenue	
Reason 2: Change in Number of Units	
Reason 3: Change in Cost	
Total Explained	X

Figure 11.2. The profit and loss view adds revenue as another variable likely to need explanation.

Unit Cost Views

Some organization styles prefer unit cost views. This may be due to user fees based on unit pricing or that the cost view provides a useful measurement for performance evaluation, trending, or both. (See Figure 11.3.)

It is also possible to use unit cost views in conjunction with simple or profit and loss views.

Unit cost views are inherently more difficult to explain. Changes in direct costs and indirect costs occur as in simple and profit and loss views. However, unit cost reconciliation explanations must also consider the impact of changes in the number of units.

The multitude of possible causes for change increases the difficulty of analyzing results. For example, an increase in number of units may hide an unfavorable cost development. A drop in number of units may offset really good cost performance.

The dynamics can get fairly complicated, and cost accounting textbooks pay significant attention to different types of variance analysis. Consider, for example, that fixed costs automatically increase on a per unit basis when units decline and automatically decrease on a per unit basis when units increase. Some of these variance analyses may be of interest to government practitioners in complex situations.

Unit Cost Results and Reconciliation

Output A	Plan or Prior	Actual	Delta
Unit Cost A			X

Reconciliation Explanation for Unit Cost Delta

Reason 1: Change in Number of Units	
Reason 2: Change in Direct Cost	
Reason 3: Change in Indirect Cost	
Total Explained	X

Figure 11.3. Unit cost explanations can be made more difficult because unit cost is a ratio of cost to output.

One difference between unit cost views and the simple or profit and loss views is that aggregation generally does not make sense. Adding unit costs of output A to outputs B and C does not make mathematical sense. Adding costs of outputs A, B, and C and dividing that sum by the total of units for outputs A, B, and C calculates an average unit cost that may not be meaningful in any operational control sense.

Measuring the number of units may also be more difficult than initially thought. Even the simplest unit cost represents an average of the actual costs for each individual unit. This is not an issue if all units are nearly identical and consume roughly the same input of resources. However, this is often not the case. Many government services may have significant differences in complexity. For example, the unit cost of putting out a fire will probably not be useful in any operational control sense because the number of fires includes small, simple, easy fires as well as difficult, large, and complex fires.

Counting the number of units may also be problematic. Some organizations simply count inputs or started units. This is less than satisfactory as a control measure because the cost incurred does not relate to the number of new inputs that presumably have received little attention and consumed little cost.

Counting completed units makes more sense, but even this can be difficult. This is especially true in long cycle time situations. Consider low-volume outputs where cycle times are long in comparison to the accounting period of interest. If the cycle time is 12 months, it is likely that unit cost for the year will vary wildly simply because of timing issues. Little learning about performance would result.

Figure 11.4 shows a hypothetical example of a 12-month cycle time process with an annual measurement schema over a 3-year period. Three starts are made in the 2nd and 11th months of the first year. Nothing gets completed in the first year, while the second year shows six completions. Unit cost calculations for these periods are effectively meaningless. Only in the third year, when start and completion occur in the same period, do we see a true reflection of work accomplished.

The solution to this problem is equivalent units analysis. This process evaluates the percentage of completion that occurred in the time period being measured. Completion percentages are added to calculate the

Timing Issues

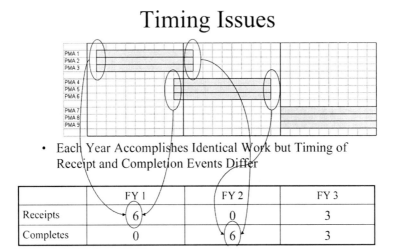

- Each Year Accomplishes Identical Work but Timing of Receipt and Completion Events Differ

	FY 1	FY 2	FY 3
Receipts	6	0	3
Completes	0	6	3

Figure 11.4. Long cycle time outputs create a special case because the timing of completion can distort performance.

number of equivalent units completed. Figure 11.5 shows how this technique works.

Equivalent units analysis calculates a better measure for an output based control process (Figure 11.5). It is useful in many circumstances, including projects. However, it suffers because the percentage of

Equivalent Units Analysis

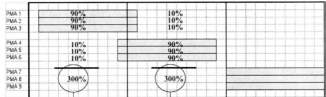

- Adds Partially Completed Pieces From Each Period to Calculate Equivalent Fully Completed Units

	FY 1	FY 2	FY 3
Receipts	6	0	3
Completes	0	6	3
Equiv Units	3	3	3

Figure 11.5. Equivalent units analysis constructs a better measure of output performance by estimating the number of fully completed equivalent units in a time period.

completion is, at best, an estimate. In fact, the percentage of completion may be completely undeterminable. In such cases, equivalent units analysis fails and a unit cost view for output based control may not be desirable.

Conclusions

Output based control processes are significantly more complex than role based or organization based processes. Given complexity variations, they also tend to be more diverse. The addition of output related effects drives both complexity and diversity.

CHAPTER 12

Bureau of Engraving and Printing

Introduction

Everybody is familiar with the product of the Bureau of Engraving and Printing (BEP)—that is, the currency of the United States. Most, however, are not familiar with the operating environment of the Bureau and how it differs from most government organizations in two significant ways.

The first difference is that, although BEP is a branch of the United States Treasury Department, it receives no appropriated funds. BEP exemplifies a type of governmental organization known as an enterprise or revolving fund. Revenues are generated by sales of products and services, and the revenues must cover both operating costs and capital requirements.

Second, BEP's culture does not assume its indefinite continuation. Unlike many government organizations, its history includes the loss of significant workload (stamp production) due to cost considerations. Furthermore, numerous other nations use commercial printers to provide their currencies.

Background and History

We have to watch the costs of the currency and stamps we produce, just like a commercial business. We have been able to hold the price to the Fed at $26 per thousand notes for the last five years because of productivity gains from new technology and innovative work practices. At the same time we were able to generate the resources to build the Fort Worth facility without any appropriations from Congress. Politics don't drive the action here, costs do.[1]

—Paul Blackmer, Assistant Director (Administration),
1990 Bureau of Engraving and Printing

In the last twenty years we have lost the stamp business to low cost competitors but we still track and manage costs of currency production. We feel a strong need to be cost effective because we feel our existence is not guaranteed. Learning from the history of the stamp program, we assume that private sector competition can replace us.

—Len Olijar, Associate Director (CFO), 2009 Bureau of Engraving and Printing

BEP's customers are not obligated by law to purchase from the Bureau. BEP used to produce all the stamps issued by the U.S. Postal Service but lost that business in the 1990s to lower cost competition. Coin production, done by the U.S. Mint, also represents a perennial competitive threat to the use of currency because printing dollar bills is roughly half of BEP's workload. The Federal Reserve System is the Bureau's predominate customer.

Originally, private bank note companies printed all U.S. currency. Security concerns raised by the Civil War initiated federal activity. In 1862, four women and two men were hired by the Treasury Department to affix seals and to sign notes printed elsewhere. The actual printing of banknotes by Treasury employees started in 1863. Created by law in 1869, the "Engraving and Printing Bureau" gradually absorbed the functions performed by the private bank note companies, and by October 1, 1877, BEP was printing all U.S. currency.

The use of U.S. postage stamps to prepay delivery fees was first authorized by law on March 3, 1847. Initially, stamps were also printed under government contract by private firms. This responsibility was assumed by the Bureau in 1894.

In 1914, the Main Bureau building was constructed in Washington, DC, and the Annex building was completed in 1938. In 1991, the Bureau opened the Western Currency Facility in Fort Worth, Texas. Comprising usable floor space of more than 25 acres, these buildings currently house 2,000 employees. (See Figure 12.1.)

Figure 12.1. Washington, DC, facility (left). Forth Worth facility (right).

BEP, by the Act of August 4, 1950 (Public Law 81-656), 31 U.S.C. 181 et seq., was authorized to operate as an enterprise fund. The Act released the bureau from the annual process of obtaining Congressional appropriations. BEP was given ownership of equipment, goods, and raw materials that were then on hand and a specified amount of working capital. BEP's fund was to be reimbursed by customer agencies for the direct and indirect costs incurred in making products and providing services. As in a private enterprise, cash inflow was to equal or exceed cash outflow; hence, the term *enterprise fund*. BEP's records were maintained on an accrual accounting basis to better match revenues with expenses.

Public Law 95-81, effective July 31, 1977, further extended BEP's financial independence by directing that BEP include in its product prices amounts to be used for future equipment acquisition and necessary increases in working capital. This law permitted the Bureau to retain prior year earnings when they were needed for planned capital investment, working capital, or both.

Cost Management History

The U.S. Postal Service's desire for lower stamp costs pushed BEP into managerial costing. The Postal Service started its effort by putting a limited number of stamp issues up for competitive bids. BEP at that time had accounting capabilities similar to most federal organizations. That is, it was only able to determine the average cost per stamp from the cost data included in required external reports.

However, average stamp costs proved disastrous in the bidding process even though they were accurate. The reason for this problem is that not all stamps are the same. Commemorative stamps have small production runs that must absorb all engraving and setup costs. Furthermore, they tend to have multiple, often complex, images. As a result, they are much more expensive to produce than the common stamp (such as flag stamps), which are mass produced in large numbers and have a single image.

Using average cost for bidding caused problems in two ways because the average falls in between the costs of high-cost commemorative and low-cost bulk stamps. BEP's average cost bid for a bulk stamp job would never win the business, as it was too high. On the other hand, average cost bids understated the cost of commemorative stamps, which BEP would win. Actually producing such a complex stamp at that cost, however, was impossible.[2] Greg Boutin, Cost Accounting Manager in 1990 and now Assistant Director of Technology, related the following:

> An adverse selection problem arises with our pricing methodology. If I overprice a stamp simply due to an inaccurate cost allocation, the Bureau could lose that job even when our actual costs are competitive. And worse, in losing that job the amount of cost that I overallocated doesn't go away. It stays with the Bureau and we lose money. But when I underestimate the cost of production, we keep those products and the revenues we receive probably don't cover our costs of production.

Solving this problem required BEP to develop much more definitive costing capabilities in order to understand the real cost incurred by different types of products. This effort was also complicated by the fact that stamps could be produced in coils, books, and sheets. Furthermore, separating the high cost of currency driven security from stamp production also pushed BEP into understanding and allocating costs on appropriate cause and effect bases.

Even though BEP no longer prints stamps, the cost management legacy remains, with the fear that currency printing could go down the same path. The result is an organization that, over the decades, has matured its ability to measure and manage the costs of its outputs.

The Money Factory

The mission statement of BEP today is "to design and manufacture high quality security documents that deter counterfeiting and meet customer requirements for quality, quantity and performance."[3]

The first step in security production is engraving a piece of soft steel, known as the master die. Each part of the design, such as the portrait, vignette, ornamentation, and lettering, is hand cut by different engraver specialists. The difficulty and artistry involved in the engraving process are the primary deterrents to counterfeiting and prerequisite to the equally difficult intaglio printing process. No other printing process possesses the fidelity of fine lines and distinctive three-dimensional effects.

The use of portraits in security design takes full advantage of the special characteristics of intaglio printing because even a slight alteration in breadth, spacing, or depth of line on the part of a counterfeit causes a perceptible facial change.

The master die is hardened and then converted into side-by-side, multiple images by a process known as *siderography*. The multiple images are converted into nickel printing plates through a plating process. The original dies are stored and can be used repeatedly. For example, the Lincoln portrait on the $5 bill was originally engraved in 1869 but was used for more than 100 years in the production of $5 notes.

BEP prints all currency on high-speed sheetfed rotary presses capable of printing up to 10,000 sheets per hour. The presses use four plates of 32 notes each. In the intaglio printing process, ink is loaded on the plate and then wiped off, leaving ink only in the recessed areas of the plate. Each sheet of paper is then forced under extremely high pressure (up to 60 tons per square inch) into the engraved recesses of the plate to pick up the ink. The surface of the bill feels slightly raised, while the reverse side feels slightly indented. Currency backs are printed in green ink in the first pass through a press, and the currency faces are printed in black ink after a 48-hour drying period.

After another drying cycle, the 32 note sheets are cut in half and each half sheet is inspected for defects. Because of the ready cash value of the product, each sheet is identified and tracked closely. Scrap, which averages less than 5%, is subject to extremely tight inventory control and physical security procedures.

In the final printing operation, the Treasury Seal, serial number, and the appropriate Federal Reserve District seal and number are overprinted on the sheet. The back end of the overprint operation also cuts, compresses, bands, and shrink-wraps the currency into bar-coded "bricks" comprising 40 stacks, each with 100 notes. At this point, although not yet officially monetized by the Federal Reserve, production is complete. The currency is placed in a vault to await shipment to one of the Federal Reserve banks. The Federal Reserve then monitors and distributes the currency through its network of member banks.

Twenty years ago, all denominations used the same inks and paper. The product was identical except for the picture. Today, each denomination of currency is different. Higher value denominations have increasingly more significant counterfeit deterrent features. These include watermarks, strips, and optically variable inks.

Currency, or Federal Reserve notes, is printed in seven denominations: $1, $2, $5, $10, $20, $50, and $100.[4] The 2008 production output of currency (in millions of notes) can be seen in Table 12.1.

BEP ended 2008 at its lowest staffing level since 1898. This can be partially attributed to operational realignment over the past 2 years, which streamlined operations, eliminated redundant functions, and combined similar activities. Staffing has also been reduced due to the introduction of new technology and more efficient production processes.

Leadership Driven Management

"High productivity, rigid quality control, and cost effectiveness" have been emphasized for years. Production processes rely heavily on automation and other advanced technologies. Meeting customer's security requirements has become increasingly important. BEP provides counterfeit and alteration deterrence through design assistance and advice, its difficult-to-duplicate printing processes, state-of-the-art detection technology, and close liaison with the Secret Service.

BEP conducts extensive research and development programs to improve the quality of products, reduce manufacturing costs, and strengthen deterrents to counterfeiting. It engraves its own dies; manufactures the necessary printing plates; provides its own security; maintains its buildings, machinery, and equipment; and stores and delivers products in

Table 12.1. 2008 Currency Production (M)

$		%
1	3,577.6	46
2	0.0	0
5	1,203.2	16
10	1,094.4	14
20	633.6	8
50	0.0	0
100	1,209.6	16
Total	7,698.4	100

accordance with the requirements of customer agencies. It even employs staff to examine and reconstruct burned or mutilated currency, which is fully replaced upon verification.

BEP's executive structure consists of the Bureau Director, a Deputy Director, six Associate Directors, and a Chief Counsel. The executive committee structure includes an Executive Committee, the Capital Investment Committee, and various planning committees and subcommittees. The planning committees and subcommittees are composed of a cross section of BEP senior and midlevel managers who represent diverse organizational units. By cutting across organizational lines, these groups serve to promote effective communication, increased collaboration, and participative, proactive management.

BEP's latest Strategic Plan (2003–2008) reflects management's objectives:

> This Strategic Plan furthers our commitment to maintaining state-of-the-art production capability, product quality and security, and employee safety and environmental stewardship as we continue to *cost effectively* meet the needs of our customers and the American public [italics added].

Furthermore, the plan goes on to state five strategic goals of the organization:

- Strategic Goal I: Customer Satisfaction. Satisfy the Federal Reserve Board and the public by providing responsive service and quality products.
- Strategic Goal II: Quality Manufacturing. Manufacture state-of-the-art currency of consistently high quality while improving productivity and cost performance.
- Strategic Goal III: Counterfeit Deterrence. Produce state-of-the-art currency that deters counterfeiting, contributes to public confidence, facilitates daily commerce, and extends the useful life of notes in circulation.
- Strategic Goal IV: Security and Accountability. Ensure an environment of comprehensive security and accountability for the Bureau's personnel, facilities, and products.

- Strategic Goal V: Resource Management. Manage Bureau resources to increase internal efficiency and effectiveness in support of the other strategic goals.

The Office of the Chief Financial Officer

The 2009 Financial Report clearly states the objective of the Office:

> The mission of the CFO Directorate is to provide superior customer service while: maintaining the integrity of the Bureau's revolving fund; executing financial management responsibilities; ensuring proper authorization for production activities; promoting compliance with internal controls, ISO standards for quality and environmental management systems and Treasury regulations; providing acquisition services, and redeeming mutilated paper currency.

This is an unusual statement of responsibility not found in most federal operations where external reporting requirements and budget consume almost all accounting effort. However, while most other organizations still struggle with the efforts required to receive a clean audit opinion, BEP almost takes them for granted. The year 2009 saw the 25th consecutive unqualified audit opinion. Furthermore, it was the fifth consecutive year in which BEP received an unqualified opinion on its internal control over financial reporting.

According to Chief Financial Officer (CFO) Len Olijar, the goal of BEP's cost management process is to find "opportunities, not problems." He sees his role as "helping the Bureau in achieving its Mission, not just in putting together numbers." Finding the right staff to help in achieving the mission is not an easy task.

> People who can put together numbers are pretty common. The person with analytic skills is much rarer. The numbers give you clues, but you have to work at it to get to the root cause: to find out the story of what is driving the numbers.

BEP has been formally managing cost for more than 20 years, so most manufacturing supervisors are familiar (and comfortable) with cost accounting asking questions and raising issues. New supervisors, however, usually quickly recognize that the cost staff is not there to "beat them up" but to help them achieve the organization's goals. Olijar adds that, in his experience, "know it all" supervisors who do not value the cost staff's input tend to fail: "those who don't listen, don't succeed."

The Office of the Chief Financial Officer has three branches to accommodate its multifunctional role. The Office of Compliance maintains the integrity of the fund and addresses internal control and audit requirements. The Office of Acquisition brings a level of financial integrity to the procurement process. The Office of Financial Management provides all managerial and financial accounting processes. These include general ledger accounting, cost accounting, payroll, budget, and financial systems.

Dan Peterson runs the Cost Accounting Branch in the Office of Financial Management. A 22-year veteran, Dan has worked at BEP since earning his bachelor's degree in business administration. The branch includes three other employees: two cost accountants and a technician.

Cost Measurement

Tables 12.2 and 12.3 show the balance sheet and operating statement of BEP for fiscal years 2007 and 2008. Direct materials, labor, and manufacturing overhead represented the majority of BEP's total cost.

The direct materials category captures the costs of paper and inks used in printing. Direct labor includes the payroll cost of employees working directly on the products. Manufacturing overhead represents expenses that are closely associated with the production process. Labor related manufacturing overhead includes FICA, unemployment insurance, and other benefit costs of direct labor and supervisory personnel. Other manufacturing overhead includes printing press depreciation, equipment power utilization, and expenses of manufacturing supplies.

Engraving and plate making activities are considered direct labor operations within BEP's cost system. Engraving activities are recorded on a job order basis to capture the costs involved in particular jobs, especially special orders. Materials used in plate manufacturing are charged to the using cost center.

Direct labor and manufacturing overhead costs are accumulated in roughly 20 cost centers. These costs are distributed to currency type by production facility on the basis of machine hours within the cost center. Material costs—paper and ink—are charged directly to the currency type.

The ability to report manufacturing costs by currency type is important because that view of cost is the one used at BEP's cost meetings. Twenty years ago, there was little difference in the cost of different denominations. Now different denominations have different papers, different security features, and significantly different costs. Furthermore, the pace of change in the product has increased, and new security features are introduced in one denomination at a time.

A considerable portion of BEP's total cost cannot be directly related to individual manufacturing processes, making it difficult to accurately attribute these expenses to product groups and products. Manufacturing Support covers activities performed in more than 100 cost centers, providing support functions such as planning, scheduling, security, facility maintenance, warehousing, and purchasing. General and Administrative costs represent functions such as financial management, personnel, information systems, and others not associated with manufacturing operations. Research and development includes the costs of new products and process enhancements, such as counterfeit deterrence. Expenses of the indirect cost centers and activities, including payroll, benefits, travel, and supplies, are accumulated and managed by the cost center.

The Precost Meetings

The formal cost management process at the BEP centers on two monthly meetings of key personnel to review the previous month's costs and performance. The first of these meetings is called the Precost Meeting. It occurs religiously 2 days before the Director's Cost Meeting, which is held the third Wednesday of the month.

This meeting is run by Dan Peterson and focuses on details of manufacturing costs. It is attended by manufacturing supervisors and superintendents. One session is held for each facility, with the meeting for Fort Worth taking place via video teleconferencing.

Costs are looked at for a number of key metrics in currency production. Spoilage, or scrap, costs are looked at for paper, black ink, green ink, black metallic ink, and overprinting ink by denomination. Spoilage costs are compared with standard and the previous month's performance to highlight variances from expectations. Standards are changed when the currency order changes.

Inks are very expensive in the currency printing process, costing up to $650 per pound. Therefore, "ink mileage" is a key cost and performance measure. Ink mileage, actually expressed as the number of sheets printed per pound, is presented by currency type. (Detailed reports can break this cost out by cost center for each type of ink by denomination.)

To aid managers in focusing on key issues, Peterson publishes an informal "highlights" report a day or two before the Precost Meeting. This report, comprising a handful of Excel file pages, pulls a few significant items out of the larger report that includes all details. Peterson provides this report to "assist the program managers in doing their jobs." He further explains that he sees his role as an information resource. "We don't want the Precost Meeting to be known as the Ambush Meeting."

The chart in Figure 12.2 is one of many from the July 2009 Precost Meeting. It shows $20 note production in the Washington, DC, facility. Brackets indicate an unfavorable cost performance. The report shows favorable areas where incurred costs were less than standard: face ink, for example, was $31,091 favorable to standard.

The report shows a very costly performance degradation in "cope pack" of ($182,093). Such an unfavorable occurrence begs the question of "why did this occur?" In this case, the "note" at the bottom of the page suggests that the answer was a "retroactive scrapping" of two lots. Note that the year-to-date performance of $4.41 (per 1,000 notes) is actually favorable to the $4.61 standard.

A number of important indicators are also provided graphically for discussion in the meeting. Such a portrayal of cost information allows the user to quickly see variations from prior time periods as well as from the standard. Figure 12.2 shows the favorable "mileage" of face ink in July that was noted earlier.

Director's Cost Meeting

The second key meeting is called the Director's Cost Meeting. It is scheduled on every executives' calendar for 1:30 p.m. every third Wednesday

STATEMENT OF CURRENCY PRODUCTION COSTS
EASTERN CURRENCY FACILITY
JULY 2009 - FY 2009

****** NEXT GENERATION CURRENCY DESIGN – $20 NOTEPRODUCTION ******

| | UNIT COST PER 1000 NOTES | | | TOTAL COST IMPACT | JULY PRODUCTION VOLUME | SHIFT PRODUCTIVITY | | | YTD ACTUAL |
OPERATION	STANDARD	ACTUAL	VARIANCE			STANDARD	JULY	YTD	
PAPER	$19.06	$19.06	$0.00	$0					$19.06
OFFSET INK	0.02	0.03	(0.01)	(908)					0.02
BACK INK	1.72	1.41	0.31	34,216					1.39
FACE INK - BLACK	1.50	1.48	0.02	1,481					1.41
FACE INK - METALLIC	0.02	0.01	0.01	740					0.01
FACE INK - OVI	1.67	1.25	0.42	31,091					1.61
OFFSET PRINT	2.80	2.30	0.50	45,415	2,860,000	47,000	47,667	32,031	4.59
PRINT BACK	2.15	2.54	(0.39)	(43,046)	3,455,019	42,000	40,175	35,894	2.69
PRINT FACE	2.32	2.51	(0.19)	(14,065)	2,318,349	39,000	40,673	35,552	2.75
	$31.26	$30.59	$0.67	$54,924					$33.53
MECH EXAM	$2.71	$3.07	($0.36)	(16,963)					$2.96
COPE PACK	4.61	8.68	(4.07)	(182,093)					4.41
COPE INK	0.63	0.62	0.01	447					0.69
NOTEPACKAGING	0.40	0.56	(0.16)	(7,168)					0.40
FRS VAULT	0.33	0.46	(0.13)	(5,824)					0.30
	$8.68	$13.39	($4.71)	($211,601)					$8.76
COST EFFECT OF SPOILAGE	1.97	1.50	0.47	23360					3.17
TOTAL CASH FLOW - RELATED COST	$41.91	$45.48	($3.57)	($133,317)					$45.46
DEPRECIATION	4.94	4.94	0.00						4.94
TOTAL MFG COST	$46.85	$50.42	($3.57)						$50.40

PRODUCTION SPOILAGE:

STANDARD	ACTUAL	PERCENT VARIANCE
5.75%	4.48%	22.10%

YTD: 8.01%

$20 NEXGEN INTAGLIO PRODUCTION BY PRESS TYPE:

	I-10	ORLOF
BACKS	0.00%	100.00%
FACES	0.00%	100.00%

NOTE: NEGATIVE NUMBERS INDICATE UNFAVORABLE VARIANCES

Figure 12.2. A sample of a report used in the after action review.

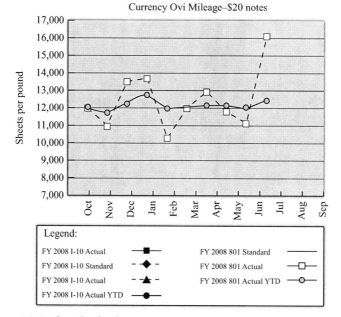

Figure 12.3. Graphs facilitate communication and learning.

of the month. It is run by the Director of the BEP and is attended by all executive level staff and their key subordinates. The data shown here are more aggregated than data at the Precost Meeting but includes both monthly and year-to-date results.

The areas covered are similar to those in the Precost Meeting. Spoilage and ink mileage by currency and facility are shown. Additionally, a cost performance section of the report shows cost per 1,000 notes for the month and year to date by facility compared with the standard. Furthermore, each facility's performance is dissected into material, labor, overhead, and volume impacts compared with the standard.

The display of volume impact is a common technique in variance analysis. BEP considers labor and depreciation as fixed costs for the purpose of calculating this variance. Larger production runs spread these costs over more notes, therefore lowering the "$ per 1,000 notes" metric. Isolating the effect of volume change allows leadership to see the other variances as representing a measure of performance efficiency.

CFO Olijar opens the meeting and gives a brief summary. Then the Chief of the Office of Financial Management, Alan Wibbenmeyer, begins going through the numbers shown in Figure 12.4. Questions from the Director, the Deputy Director, the CFO, and others soon begin. Most questions are answered by the manufacturing managers from the Fort Worth and Washington facilities or their staffs. Questions often center on the root causes of observed variances, the implemented corrective actions, and the month-to-date indicators that might signal a turnaround.

In July, the Western Currency Facility in Fort Worth showed a very large, but favorable, year-to-date total cost variance of $2.4 million. This variance is broken out into its causes by further analysis shown on the bottom of the first page of the report. Here it can be seen that higher than expected production volume caused $1.3 million of the favorableness, with labor also posting $0.9 million favorable. The purpose of the Director's Cost Meeting is for all to learn the reasons for these unexpected results.

Delivery status is also shown in terms of the number days ahead or behind schedule by facility. The meeting closes with a discussion of indirect costs. These are presented by area, with a comparison of actual costs incurred year to date and the budget for that same period. These numbers seem to change infrequently and are primarily due to overtime variation.

The complete manufacturing report used in the July 2009 Director's Cost Meeting is shown in Figure 12.4 as "Production Cost and Quality Report." The entire meeting took 30–40 minutes.

The Future of Cost Management at BEP

Increasingly sophisticated security measures and the expanded use of machines to authenticate currency in the retail environment are driving BEP to significantly reduce product variability and raise overall product quality. It is no longer acceptable for currency quality to be determined solely by appearance; it must also function in the automated environment increasingly seen in retail establishments. The stringent quality demands for currency in person-to-machine transactions will undoubtedly increase the importance of accurate product cost information, as well as cost management and control for the foreseeable future.

PRODUCTION COST AND QUALITY REPORT
JULY 2009

QUALITY:			BPS Tested	Passed	Wait/Hold
		WCF	47	46	1
1 process on hold from prior perio	ECF		41	41	0

COST PERFORMANCE:			Cost per 1000 notes	Cost Impact
	WCF	Current Month Cost (Above) or Below Standard	($0.4464)	($134,272)
		YTD Total Cost (Above) or Below Standard	$0.7151	$2,425,728
	ECF	Current Month Cost (Above) or Below Standard	($1.3342)	($204,928)
		YTD Cost (Above) or Below Standard	$0.1272	$288,480
	Total	Current Month Cost (Above) or Below Standard	($0.7465)	($339,200)
		YTD Cost (Above) or Below Standard	$0.4795	$2,714,208

BREAKDOWN OF YTD COST :				Cost Impact
	WCF	Material Cost (Above) or Below Standard		$201,732
		Labor Cost (Above) or Below Standard		$853,196
		Overhead Cost (Above) or Below Standard		$64,470
		Volume Impact (Above) or Below Standard		$1,306,330
		Total MFG Cost (Above) or Below Standard		$2,425,728
	ECF	Material Cost (Above) or Below Standard		$246,509
		Labor Cost (Above) or Below Standard		$464,780
		Overhead Cost (Above) or Below Standard		($257,846)
		Volume Impact (Above) or Below Standard		($164,963)
		Total MFG Cost (Above) or Below Standard		$288,480

Figure 12.4. Director's cost meeting (continued on next page).

SPOILAGE:			Denom	Annual Standard	Month Standard	Month Actual	Last Month Actual	YTD Actual
	WCF		$1.00	3.4%		2.4%	2.9%	3.0%
		NXG	$5.00	5.5%		N/A	N/A	6.6%
		NXG	$10.00	5.0%		N/A	N/A	5.5%
		NXG	$20.00	5.5%		N/A	N/A	6.6%
		NXG	$50.00	5.0%		N/A	N/A	5.9%
		NXG	$100.00	0.0%		N/A	N/A	N/A
	ECF		$1.00	4.0%		N/A	N/A	6.0%
		NXG	$20.00	5.8%		4.5%	6.2%	8.0%
		NXG	$100.00	0.0%		N/A	N/A	N/A
		NCD	$100.00	5.4%		5.6%	5.4%	4.8%
		REG		3.4%	3.4%	2.4%	2.9%	3.2%
		NCD		5.4%	5.4%	5.6%	5.4%	4.8%
		NXG		5.4%	5.8%	4.5%	6.2%	6.7%
		Total		4.6%	4.1%	3.4%	4.0%	4.6%

INK MILEAGE:								
ECF:		Standard	Actual	YTD	WCF:	Standard	Actual	YTD
Green		95	110	107	Green	102	92	101
Black		82	84	84	Black	101	94	104
OVI	$20	12,000	16,086	12,444	$10	18,000	N/A	18,885
NCD	$100	5,845	5,489	5,339	$20	11,700	N/A	13,498
					$50	17,300	N/A	18,906
TAG	GRN	22,500	29,167	25,823				
TAG	BLK	27,000	26,000	22,650	BLK	27,000	N/A	26,134

CURRENCY DELIVERIES:			**********	MONTHLY	**********			
		Order 09	Delivered	Order	Standard	Actual	Days ahead(behind)	
ECF		2.6368	86.0%	0.2272	0.2307	0.1536	8.5	
WCF		3.8464	88.2%	0.2368	0.3366	0.2944	13.6	

Figure 12.4. Director's cost meeting (continued).

Table 12.2. Bureau of Engraving and Printing Balance Sheets

As of September 30, 2008 and 2007	2008 ($M)	2007 ($M)
Assets		
Cash	153.5	176.0
Accounts Receivable	46.6	39.1
Inventories	104.0	
Prepaid Expenses	4.9	5.5
Total Current Assets	308.9	327.7
Property and Equipment	281.9	256.1
Other Assets	18.1	18.5
Total Assets	608.8	602.2
Liabilities		
Current Liabilities		
Accounts Payable	13.4	15.5
Accrued Liabilities	28.6	29.3
Advances	6.5	1.6
Total Current Liabilities	48.4	46.4
Workers' Compensation	61.4	57.4
Total Liabilities	109.9	103.9
Equity		
Invested Capital	32.4	32.4
Cumulative Results of Operations	466.5	465.9
Total Equity	499.0	498.3
Liabilities + Equity	608.8	602.2

Table 12.3. Bureau of Engraving and Printing Statements of Operations and Cumulative Results of Operations

For the Years Ended September 30, 2008 and 2007	2008	2007
	($M)	($M)
Revenue from Sales	516.6	578.1
Cost of Goods Sold	443.3	461.6
Gross Margin	73.3	116.5
Operating Costs		
General and Administrative	60.3	56.2
Research and Development	12.4	14.0
Total	72.7	70.2
Excess of revenues over expenses	0.6	46.3

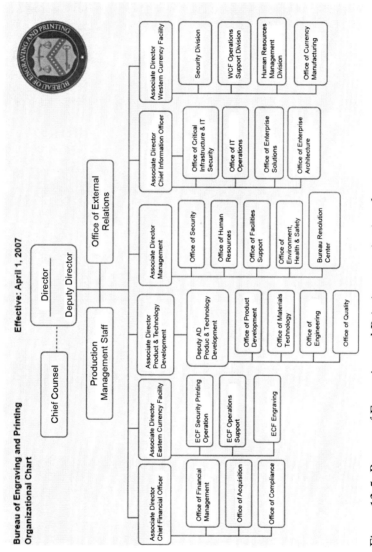

Figure 12.5. Bureau of Engraving and Printing organization chart.

PART III

Stage III Cost Use
Creating Cost Managed Enterprises

Cost managed government organizations are a good thing. They drive continuous improvement through organization based, role based, or output based cost reviews. Cost managed government enterprises build from a base of cost managed organizations to create a large-scale, multiorganization, cost controlled entity: a government enterprise.

Unfortunately, writing about this concept will be hypothetical. None exists as far as I know. However, there is no reason they cannot exist with increased interest in cost managed organization development. It is perhaps only a matter of time. The purpose of this section will be to speculate about what the cost managed enterprise might look like.

Universal Use of Cost Information

The cost managed enterprise will extensively use cost information as part of its operations. There may even be multiple views of cost information to satisfy the information needs of different purposes or functions. It will probably also have matrixed organization structures where costs are looked at from organizational as well as cross-organizational views. (See Figure 13.1.)

It is likely that the cost managed enterprise will have cost managed organizations employing organization based processes as part of their organization structure. Overhead or support elements would also participate in the role based control process. Furthermore, the enterprise would be able to redefine its costing to simultaneously support an output based view that may even cross many organization boundaries.

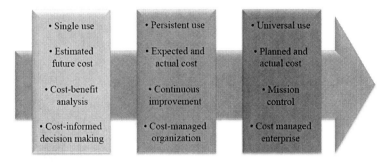

Figure 13.1. Cost managed enterprises use financial controls as a key component of accomplishing their missions because "dollars" is the language of management.

Planned and Actual Cost

Planned cost is a little different than the expected cost needed to drive a cost managed organization. Expected cost can be derived by looking at past performance or by making a model. Planned cost is a serious performance commitment. Manager/leaders build their plans and commit to their achievement. Frequently missing planned commitment is considered a significant problem in the ability of the manager/leader. Cost managed enterprises do not tolerate a manager who cannot make his plan happen.

Cost Control

Cost control means "no surprises." Cost controlled enterprises are so attuned to the costs that major surprises seldom occur. Planned commitments are carefully made and costs are thoroughly understood. Unplanned cost variances get a great deal of attention rapidly.

CHAPTER 13

Implementation Issues

Starting Point: Senior Leadership Driven Management

Leadership responsibilities in *sustaining* leadership driven management are critical. Leadership responsibilities in *creating* a leadership driven management process are indispensable.

The starting point of creating a cost managed enterprise is obviously senior leadership. Without strongly committed senior leadership, it is unlikely that any organization can be transformed into a cost managed enterprise, breaking away from decades of past practice.

There is no middle ground here. "Committed" or "interested" senior leadership is simply not good enough to overcome organizational inertia and resistance. The following implementation suggestions and, in fact, this entire work are provided for the "strongly committed" group. The suggested strategy for the "not strongly committed" group is not to implement. To attempt implementation without strongly committed senior leadership would be a waste of time and resources.

Senior leadership has two very important roles in transformation:

1. Lead immediate subordinates in the right direction and insist that they do the same with their subordinates.
2. Fund the up-front costs of transformation.

Leadership Issues in Transformation

The transition to a control process creates numerous culture change issues. Foremost is the perceived threat to managers who have not previously been accountable for cost. The vast majority of managers fall into this category in most organizations. Most will be unsure of their abilities in this area. Many will be defensive about their performance. A few will fail.

A few will be enthusiastic from the beginning and a few will openly rebel. Most will passively acquiesce. The most important task of leadership is to motivate the willing but unsure and develop them into competent managers.

While many feel that government has "too many chiefs and not enough indians," the opposite may be true in the cost management and control arena. Power and policy have been so centralized for so long that most managers below the top headquarters level think of themselves as subordinates. These managers' careers have progressed on their strengths in compliance.

The most important culture change elements will be to energize the chain of command to the point where managers at all levels recognize that they are managers of the levels below in addition to being subordinate to the level above. Leadership driven management should permeate the organization.

This will not happen without senior leadership drive. It is therefore important that senior leadership stay "on message," as their commitment will be constantly assessed by subordinates. *Signaling* is recognized as one of any senior executive's major tasks. Leadership's commitment will be tested and the entire organization will be watching. Compromising with a recalcitrant subordinate sends one message. Replacing that subordinate sends another.

Funding Transformation

As discussed earlier, the goal of leadership driven management control is not merely for program value to break even with program costs. This program should represent an investment with at least a 10 to 1 return. Resources, therefore, must be carefully planned and managed to limit the cost side of the equation while seeking maximum benefits.

We have discussed the four requirements for success: (a) leadership, (b) process, (c) analytic cost expert (ACE) staff, and (d) measurement. Now we can think about the resourcing needed in these areas.

Historically, most attempts at improving cost management in the Federal Government have allocated most, if not all, resources to the measurement effort. The needs for spending on leadership, process, and ACE staff were largely unrecognized, unfunded, and unaddressed.

It has been the thesis here that measurement may be the least important of these four requirements: leadership, process, staff, and measurement. It should be clear that leadership is the most important element in a leadership driven management control approach. However, the approach adds responsibility to existing personnel, rather than adding more personnel.

The process, similarly, requires few if any resources, as it is primarily a method of operation. Of course, leaders and ACE staff will spend time preparing, and there will be some minor costs of copies, for example, but there is no need to budget robust resources specifically for the process.

Building and training the staff of ACEs will represent the largest incremental funding commitment. The ACE staff will be a permanent addition to the organization. These positions demand highly skilled personnel who will interact with leaders at all levels of the organization.

There certainly will be some measurement cost involved in programming reports, building models, or developing new insights. These should not be large, and as recommended elsewhere, an evolutionary approach is recommended that will also have the effect of minimizing these costs.

Temporary Start-Up Costs

The largest element of unique start-up costs will undoubtedly be training. Significant training will be needed throughout the chain of command and for the ACE staff. Management training should address the needed skill set, the cultural imperatives, and the expected leadership qualities. ACE staff training should not only include the management elements but also add more technical issues of cost analysis.

Another major start-up cost will be the need to staff a transition office. This office should be placed high in the organization supporting senior leaders in implementing the cultural changes. This office should phase out after 2 or 3 years, with its personnel being ideal candidates for key ACE staff or leadership positions.

There will also be some measurement related cost at start-up. It is expected that the costs will be tightly controlled initially, with changes restricted until the process matures and leaders become skilled in specifying their requirements.

A Funding Template for Organization Based Control Transformation

Let's imagine an organization with a $1 billion annual budget. If the program goal is a modest 2% annual improvement, we should expect $20 million per year in improvements. Using the 10 to 1 ratio of benefits-to-costs limits program execution in the sustainment mode to $2 million per year. Temporary start-up costs might be expected to add an additional $2 million to the first year and $1 million to the second year. Let us consider how these resources might be distributed during the first 3 years.

Given the suggested $4 million, $3 million, $2 million budget levels yields the following year-to-year expenditure plan in constant dollars.

Table 13.1. Organization Based Control Transformation Effort Template

Percentage of Budget	First Year (%)	Second Year (%)	Third Year (%)
Leader Training	20	13	
ACE Staff Training	10	7	
Transition Office	15	10	
ACE Staff	50	67	100
Measurement Improvement	5	3	
Total	100	100	100

Table 13.2. Organization Based Control Transformation Funding Template

$K	First Year	Second Year	Third Year
Leader Training	800	400	
ACE Staff Training	400	200	
Transition Office	600	300	
ACE Staff	2,000	2,000	2,000
Measurement Improvement	200	100	
Total	4,000	3,000	2,000

A Funding Template for Role Based Control Transformation

Being significantly smaller in scope, role based control processes need significantly smaller resource levels. Let's consider that the organization spending $1 billion per year has some $300 million in annual support costs.

A 2% savings yields $6 million per year and the 10 to 1 ratio suggests that $600,000 per year would be available to support the role based control process. Training requirements would be considerably reduced because of the fewer number of people involved. Furthermore, the culture change dimension is likewise reduced for the same reason: eliminating the need for a transition office. Temporary start-up cost would be small.

It is harder to speculate on the funding needs for an output based, cost managed organization. This is because output based control processes will probably have a lot of diversity. Each will require a "custom fit" of measurements and processes. If existing cost measurement can support the needed reporting, it is likely that the funding suggested for organization based control might be reasonable.

Benefits and Methods for Valuing Them

The 2% benchmarks used previously are probably very conservative, particularly in the first few years as "low hanging fruit" is harvested. Productivity improvement statistics in the U.S. manufacturing sector typically run two to three times this level. The manufacturing sector control processes are undoubtedly very mature in comparison to government sector control processes. The 2% target should be readily achievable.

Table 13.3. Role Based Control Transformation Funding Template

$K	First Year	Second Year	Third Year
Leader Training	100	50	
ACE Staff Training	100	50	
Transition Office			
ACE Staff	600	600	600
Measurement Improvement			
Total	800	700	600

Furthermore, the 2% program counts only "hard dollar" savings. These are readily determinable cost reductions that result from contract modifications, cuts in consumption, or staff reduction. This type of benefit can be readily calculated and hard dollars rapidly reprogrammed or redirected to critical, but unfunded, mission needs.

Consider the $1 billion per year organization that implements an organization based control process. Note that after 10 years even this modest 2% goal brings in $177 million[1] of improvements: enough to represent a significant increase in mission effectiveness. A 3% annual productivity improvement yields $277 million of improvement, and a 4% annual productivity improvement yields $377 million if program budget stays as defined earlier. These are large achievements worthy of senior leadership attention.

However, hard dollar savings probably represent only a small proportion of program benefits. Cost avoidances, for example, are typically much larger. While not counting toward the 2% goal, cost avoidances will frequently occur as leaders become more forward looking and better at planning. Cost avoidances cannot be reprogrammed and, in most cases, can only be estimated. Nevertheless, they are a significant benefit, and some effort should be made to track them and to acknowledge their mission contribution.

Finally, there is a third category of program benefit that is usually even more ambiguous. These results can best be described as quality improvements. There may not be a hard dollar saving or even a cost avoidance, but something is changed in the process that results in better service or output toward mission goals. These should also be valued even if the estimation methodology is crude, as this category also represents improvements that should be valued and desired.

It would not be surprising if estimated cost avoidances ran two to three times the calculated value of "hard dollar" cost savings. Furthermore, it is likely that the crudely estimated value of quality improvement exceeds that of cost avoidances.

The sum of cost savings, cost avoidances, and the value of quality improvements over the 10-year period probably comes close to the entire cost of the organization. Such a cost managed organization has undoubtedly increased its mission effectiveness: the ultimate goal of leadership driven management.

CHAPTER 14

Conclusions

The Problem

Government organizations spend enormous amounts of money. They employ a large percentage of the workforce. They have an undeniably huge impact on the national economy and wealth. Yet they are, for the most part, unmanaged.

What passes for management is a combination of oversight and audit. Oversight is primarily reactive, offering negative feedback for failures and demanding additional rules and regulations to prevent reoccurrences. Audits look for "bright line" discrepancies and clear violations to those rules and regulations. Working in tandem, these processes provide indignant sound bites and the appearance of management that is really mindless compliance to rules.

Government operations are often criticized for "waste and mismanagement."

Yet the current situation, unfortunately, can best be described as one of "unmanagement" rather than "mismanagement."

The Solution

Government organizations need better financial management control processes to accomplish their missions in the environment of constrained fiscal resources. Such processes would shift management behavior from defensive, problem avoidance mode, to aggressive improvement and efficiency oriented action.

The leadership driven management control processes described in this book fit the need. They create well-defined accountability and institutionalize disciplined, periodic performance reviews. These powerful mechanisms do not eliminate errors and problems. In fact, compared with current practice they should expose many issues. This is not a bad thing. It is (or should be) a good thing to find problems, fix them, and learn from the experience.

The goal of this book has been to define practical applications for financial management control processes in government. Furthermore, it has sought to define the critical requirements for success with the hope of speeding transformation to a new environment of aggressive, proactive, continuously improving government organizations. The long-term success at Fort Huachuca, SSC Pacific, and the Bureau of Engraving and Printing suggests that leadership driven management can be a persistent force rather than a temporary management fad.

Challenge: Culture Change

The desired outcome is a culture in which simply spending 99.9% of the budget no longer constitutes good financial management. This desire recognizes that continuous improvement in efficiency leads to continuous improvement in mission effectiveness.

This is a difficult task. It inherently requires sound, but subjective, judgments. The problem with judgment is that legitimate differences of opinion exist. There is no single correct answer or method. It is impossible to write a procedure, operating manual, regulation, or law that will adequately cover a socially complex problem such as child rearing, war fighting, or financial management.

Guidelines, theories, and doctrines can help the process, but ultimately, subjective judgment is inescapable. It also seems likely that consensus on good, but subjective, judgment is more difficult in a highly charged and political environment.

Challenge: Constructive Critique

The relative openness of government processes combined with inherently adversarial oversight and audit make leader judgments easy targets for criticism. Management is inherently subjective since decisions require judgment and judgment is never infallible. Furthermore, it is *always* possible to criticize judgment and usually from many directions.

This leads to a lot of defensive, compliance, and avoidance behavior. It may be responsible for much of the lack of clarity in government financial reporting. It may also explain the lack of clear financial management accountability embedded in many organization structures.

Critics must recognize that the goal of a good financial control process is to uncover problems in order to fix them. A well-controlled organization with very effective learning processes can easily be made to look bad simply by "exposing" the problems found. In fact, the best organizations would look to be the worst. Perhaps cost information and the workings of the leadership driven management processes should be government proprietary information, not fodder to gain political points or media ratings.

Challenge: Education and Training

There is a significant need to reeducate a lot of people. All existing training programs should modify their programs of instruction as appropriate to include cost measurement, management, and control issues. All leaders, including senior leaders, in the cost chain of command need training as part of the transformation process.

Colleges and universities also need to rethink their curricula. Public Administration programs, in particular, must expand their interest beyond traditional policy and political issues to include internal administration. Business Administration programs would be wise to think of their offerings in the broader context of "management," rather than defining themselves as only "business" schools.

Challenge: Congressional Leadership

Congress might become a real force for better management of government. This opportunity is due to its position at the top of the financial management hierarchy. It controls the purse strings. It could do much to improve control of spending.

Congress could help promote the needed change by rewriting some of the rules and laws. Perhaps the Anti-Deficiency Act should be questioned. The time and cost of imposing budget control should be questioned, particularly at lower levels of the organization hierarchy. Even if Congress did not modify the law's requirement, agencies should feel empowered to substitute leadership driven management control for budget control mechanisms at lower levels on the organization chart.

Changing budget law permitting agencies to carry over a small percentage of their appropriations from one year to the next might also make sense. Such permission would discourage much of the spending that occurs annually at the end of the fiscal year as organizations scramble to spend. The change would promote better spending of these funds by removing the time pressure to spend the funds or else "lose" them.

Allowing and even encouraging the reprogramming and redirection of savings would have a similar effect. Currently, funds can get locked into accounts and organizations that may not need them. Using funds more wisely should be encouraged, not discouraged, as we seek to empower leaders while holding them more accountable for operational improvement.

Expanding budget appropriations beyond the current year could eliminate much of the angst and effort spent on budget formulation and defense. This change would involve tremendous political issues that begin to impact the checks and balances role of Congress, but perhaps a practical compromise is in order. It seems strange that the most powerful and stable government in the world has a built-in, annual, self-inflicted financial crisis.

For example, maybe the second year would be appropriated at only 90% of the current year and the third year at 75% or 80%. At the department or agency level, it would be hard to imagine changes greater than these in all but the most extreme cases. Of course, Congress would always have the prerogative to renege on a second- or third-year budget, but the stability provided in most cases would do much to improve the culture of continuous improvement in financial management.

Government agencies could accomplish much of the same effect by allowing lower levels of the organization to plan on multiyear horizons. Certainly, contracts can be written with "escape clauses" that ensure that only Congressionally approved budget dollars can be spent. This should pose few practical problems while preserving Congressional prerogatives.

Finally, Congress might charter the Government Accountability Office to expand its traditional role as watchdog and auditor. It could be a real force for constructive critique as well as an aid in the transformation process.

Challenge: Developing Cost Effective Accountability Mechanisms

Much of what is reported as accounting problems in government are really accountability issues. When managers are truly accountable for the numbers, the problems do not get so bad for two reasons. First, accounting mistakes, that is, measurement errors, do not accumulate if managers actively monitor them. They get fixed promptly. Second, managers are more likely to take timely action to fix real operational problems accurately reported by the accounting process before a problem becomes a crisis.

Leadership should review, approve, and monitor the responsibilities and performance of all key subordinates. For example, who, by name and title, is responsible for what? Although this sounds simple, it can be difficult to define this chain of command in a large government organization. Often it is unclear who is in charge when military personnel, for example, are funded by one mechanism, ammunition by another, and support functions by yet another. The various flavors of support functions may each have committees and proponents and staff organizations that all seem to have some power but little accountability.

Senior leaders should also value their role in the after action review at the top of the hierarchy. The after action review is a meeting in which operating managers present financial results in comparison to their previously planned commitments. This dynamic feedback mechanism provides accountability throughout the organization when it occurs at all levels within the chain of command hierarchy.

Challenge: Motivating Change

Quarterly public meetings to review the best continuous improvement initiatives within an agency would provide tremendous positive motivation. Perhaps there could be a number of different categories of review, such as savings or improvements by contractors, purchase price improvements, process improvements, and so forth, or even customer service improvements and quality enhancements. Each meeting should result in selecting the "best of the best" in each category. Personal recognition is a powerful motivator.

The objective here is to create an atmosphere of positive expectations for productivity improvement. This approach stands in stark contrast to the traditional hearing process of exposing and publicizing failure: perhaps a root cause of much of the public's lack of confidence and mistrust in government.

Challenge: Developing Useful, Credible, Affordable Financial Information Systems

Many federal agencies have little cost information available. Their accounting systems are designed to meet the need to avoid overspending budget. Newer systems and enhancements to older systems have been designed to improve external reporting capabilities. In many cases, the result does not improve the ability of operating management throughout the organization to better control operations.

Besides the need for management information systems, federal organizations also need accounting professionals who can process data into information useful for management action. These management accountants seem to be rare in the Federal Government. Their training and development represents a high-priority need.

Paradoxically, perhaps the best way to provide resources for internal management information development would be to reduce the requirements Congress imposes for external reporting. It would probably be a worthwhile investment to drastically cut the existing reporting burden on federal organizations if this effort can be applied to improving internal management information.

Challenge: Continuing Research

How can financial resources be better used to accomplish the missions of government? This is a complex issue and a blend of at least three academic disciplines: (a) economics, (b) sociology, and (c) psychology. Furthermore, it requires a practical engineering-like application of these sciences to achieve positive results.

Relatively little management research has been done in government. Corporate management has dominated the academic agenda. Companies and alumni have funded many endowed faculty chairs and sponsored much research. Business schools in general have avoided the management issues of government, and most public administration programs are taught from universities' political science departments and emphasize policy over process.

There is much to learn about management in the government sector and there is no organized mechanism to fund it. Yet the Federal Government funds much basic scientific research. Perhaps, a federally funded Research and Development Center focused on these issues would pay huge dividends.

Challenge: Building the Support Staff

Government leaders and employees are inherently as good as any in the private sector. However, their experience has not involved cost management and control. They need help.

Building a strong organization of strong Analytic Cost Experts (ACEs) is the most important transformation issue. In general, this staff does not currently exist. It must be carefully, but quickly, built to enable leadership to become truly effective financial leaders.

Challenge: Leadership, the Critical Requirement

The requirements for success begin with senior leadership because management control is fundamentally a leadership driven process and not an accounting process. Nothing is going to happen, nothing is going to change, and nothing is going to last unless leaders recognize and accept their primacy in making things happen, change, and last.

Where are the leaders who can make this happen?

They are everywhere. Everyone is a leader, a supervisor, or a manager of the activities, people, and resources under his or her authority. This is true even for the sole contributor managing himself.

Senior leaders, however, have the sole responsibility to initiate this change. Only senior leadership has the ability to direct resources and subordinates in ways that drive better resource management. Most have dedicated their lives to the missions of their organizations, and many will come to see that leadership driven management provides an opportunity to leave a lasting legacy of significance.

Conclusions

Government represents a huge piece of the domestic economy, and improving cost effectiveness in government offers significant national benefits. Politics and the democratic process can best make the tough decision between guns and butter, for example. Improved cost effectiveness in providing guns and butter, however, means that we can have more of either or both.

Who could be opposed to these outcomes? Cost effectiveness is neither Democrat nor Republican, pro-life or pro-choice, or liberal or conservative.

Current financial management processes seemed optimal for preventing large cash losses through fraud and malfeasance. Traditional oversight review will remain a powerful force in preventing gross abuse. However, micromanagement through oversight will generate headlines but not headway in continuously improving the efficiency of government.

Leadership driven management can provide continuous process improvement in the Federal Government. Perhaps a 2%, 3%, or 4% annual savings may seem insignificant to politicians and political appointees when considering the next election or short-term employment. However, sustained improvements of 2%, 3%, or 4% each year for 10 years are significant and possible.

Government leaders would be wise to place a greater proportion of their energy into leadership driven management. There is much that can be done and much progress to be made. Perhaps the needed operating philosophy could be summed up as "do ask, don't yell."

Notes

Introduction

1. Some government entities receive cash inflows from the sale of goods or services to other government entities or the public. These are called revolving funds, enterprise funds, working capital funds, industrial funds, or internal service funds. A public utility is a typical example in which user fees provide budget input. Some government organizations, such as public transportation or the Food and Drug Administration, receive a combination of appropriated funds and user fees. These organizations are also budget driven and would benefit from the concepts of this book. They will not be differentiated from organizations funded entirely by appropriation.

Chapter 1

1. Most examples from this point will focus on federal organizations and federal practice. Applicability of the concepts to state and local government organizations should be strong.

2. Chief Financial Officers Act of 1990, Public Law 101–576, 101st Cong. (1990, November 15). Emphasis added.

3. For more information on this subject, see Geiger, D. R. (1998). Practical issues in managerial cost accounting. *Government Accountants Journal, 47*(2).

4. Garrison operations have been characterized as similar to city management functions of many municipalities. It includes all the infrastructure maintenance of an Army installation.

5. See Geiger, D. R. (2000). *Winning the cost war: Applying battlefield management doctrine to the management government.* Lincoln, NE: iUniverse.com Publishing Services

Chapter 2

1. See Geiger, D. (2008, summer). New directions for cost reporting. *The Armed Forces Comptroller, 53*(3).

2. Horngren, C., Datar, S., Forster, G., Rajan, M., & Ittner, C. (2008). *Cost accounting: A managerial emphasis*. 13th ed. Upper Saddle River, NJ: Pearson Prentice Hall.

Chapter 4

1. See http://www.arcent.army.mil/mission/index.asp

2. "Theater Strategic Financial Management Initiatives," unclassified, June 2009, unpublished document, McGhee, BG Phillip, Anvari, Mort, and staff.

Chapter 5

1. In fact, even though lions are the apex predator, their hunts are only successful in about 1 of 8 attempts. Nature deals harshly with failure to achieve this success rate. As they say, "It's a jungle out there."

2. Osborne, D., & Gabler, T. (1992). *Reinventing government*. Reading, MA: Addison-Wesley, p. 9.

3. Geiger, G. R. (2000). *Winning the cost war: Applying battlefield management doctrine to the management government*. Lincoln, NE: iUniverse.com Publishing Services.

Chapter 6

1. Geiger, D. R. (2000). *Winning the cost war: Applying battlefield management doctrine to the management government*. Lincoln, NE: iUniverse.com Publishing Services.

Chapter 8

1. At the beginning of this story, the garrison commander, normally a colonel, reported to the installation commander, a major general in this case. (Subsequently, the Army has created an independent organization: the Installation Management Command.) The garrison commander is roughly equivalent to the city manager of a fair-sized city. He manages functions of contracting, logistics, facility engineering, public safety, fire protection, information systems, and morale, welfare, and recreation.

2. For more information on cost based management, see Geiger, D. R. (2000). *Winning the cost war: Applying battlefield management doctrine to the management government*. Lincoln, NE: iUniverse.com Publishing Services.

Chapter 9

1. As in many management cases, exceptions exist. Sometimes the negative consequences of reduced consumption lead to other distribution methods. See chapter 11 for examples.

2. See http://www.navyenterprise.navy.mil/about/why.aspx

3. See http://www.navyenterprise.navy.mil/index.aspx

Chapter 10

1. See http://www.spawar.navy.mil

2. Division 30 was located in Warminster, Pennsylvania, and occupied no facilities in San Diego. It had been charged millions of dollars per year for years. At the time of the meeting, it was in the process of being closed, perhaps because of its overstated costs.

3. Most government organizations are appropriated. In those organizations, the support functions would own their own budget and not pass on any cost to their customer.

4. There may be other functions that could be considered as a second step in the step down allocation process. Information systems, for example, that are primarily consumed by other staff organizations such as accounting and procurement might be good candidates for a second level step. See chapter 9 for more on step down allocation.

Chapter 11

1. Volume variance is commonly explained in cost accounting textbooks. Note that, while higher output volume raises cost, unit cost declines as fixed cost is spread over a greater number of units.

Chapter 12

1. The foundation of this chapter relies heavily on *The Bureau of Engraving: Determining the True Cost of Money (A)*, a teaching case from the Harvard Business School prepared by Dale Geiger, a doctoral student, under the supervision of Professors Robert S. Kaplan and Herman Leonard, Boston, Massachusetts, 1990.

2. In 1990, for example, costs were $1.12 per thousand for regular sheet flag stamps and about $4.00 for commemoratives. The average price was $2.15 per thousand stamps.

3. See www.bep.treas.gov

4. In 1969, printing of currency notes larger than $100 was stopped. Circulating $500, $1,000, $5,000, and $10,000 notes were retired as received in Federal Reserve banks. Two- and fifty-dollar bills are not printed annually.

Chapter 13

1. Calculated as $200 million of savings to be redirected less $2 million per year of sustainment cost and $3 million of temporary start-up cost.

Index

Note: *f* and *t* after a page number indicate a figure or table, respectively.

Announcing the Business Expert Press Digital Library
Concise E-books Business Students Need
for Classroom and Research

This book can also be purchased in an e-book collection by your library as

- a one-time purchase,
- that is owned forever,
- allows for simultaneous readers,
- has no restrictions on printing, and
- can be downloaded as PDFs from within the library community.

Our digital library collections are a great solution to beat the rising cost of textbooks. E-books can be loaded into their course management systems or onto student's e-book readers.

The **Business Expert Press** digital libraries are very affordable, with no obligation to buy in future years.

For more information, please visit **www.businessexpert.com/libraries**. To set up a trial in the United States, please contact **Sheri Allen** at *sheri.allen@globalepress.com*; for all other regions, contact **Nicole Lee** at *nicole.lee@igroupnet.com*.

OTHER TITLES IN OUR
MANAGERIAL ACCOUNTING COLLECTION
Series Editor: **Kenneth A. Merchant**

CPSIA information can be obtained at www.ICGtesting.com
Printed in the USA
BVOW011504131011

273538BV00004B/6/P